ISBN 0-8057-6936-6

Agatha Christie

Officially made a Dame of the British Empire in 1971, Agatha Christie had already reigned as queen of the classic British detective novel for a full half-century. Her extensive oeuvre of fiction continues to delight readers in both the United States and Europe: scarcely a house can be found in the English-reading world that does not contain at least one of her novels. In Hercule Poirot and Miss Marple, Christie has created two of the most memorable and beloved sleuths in all of detective fiction. Several of her novels have been produced as major motion pictures, including *Murder on the Orient Express* and *Death on the Nile,* and her play *The Mousetrap* is one of the longest-running productions in the history of the London stage.

Mary Wagoner's book is the first comprehensive overview of the Christie canon. Wagoner gracefully integrates important biographical information about the novelist into her criticism, showing clearly for the first time how Christie's work reflects her own cultural background, era, and class. *Agatha Christie* provides in-depth analyses of individual novels, locating books such as *The Murder of Roger Ackroyd* and *The Mysterious Affair at Styles* within several subcategories of Christie's fiction. Inspired by her subject's own careful writing and logical conclusions, Wagoner methodically untangles the complex web of recurring patterns and formulas in Christie's work, revealing the novelist's long-standing fascination with adapting classic

Agatha Christie
(1890–1976)

Photograph by Angus McBean, London
Reproduced by permission of Dodd, Mead & Company, Inc.

Agatha Christie

Twayne's English Authors Series

Kinley E. Roby, Editor

Northeastern University

TEAS 432

Agatha Christie

By Mary S. Wagoner

University of New Orleans

Twayne Publishers
A Division of G.K. Hall & Co. • *Boston*

Agatha Christie

Mary S. Wagoner

Copyright © 1986 by G.K. Hall & Co.
All Rights Reserved
Published by Twayne Publishers
A Division of G.K. Hall & Co.
70 Lincoln Street
Boston, Massachusetts 02111

Selections from Agatha Christie's autobiography:
Reprinted by permission of DODD, MEAD & COMPANY, INC. from *Agatha Christie: An Autobiography*. Copyright © 1977 by Agatha Christie Limited.

Copyediting supervised by Lewis DeSimone
Book production by Marne B. Sultz
Book design by Barbara Anderson

Typeset in 11 pt. Garamond
by P&M Typesetting, Inc., Waterbury, Connecticut

Printed on permanent/durable acid-free paper
and bound in the United States of America

Library of Congress Cataloging in Publication Data

Wagoner, Mary.
  Agatha Christie.

  (Twayne's English authors series; TEAS 432)
  Bibliography: p. 151
  Includes index.
  1. Christie, Agatha, 1890–1976—Criticism and interpretation. 2. Detective and mystery stories, English—History and criticism. I. Title. II. Series.
PR6005.H66Z95   1986   823'.912   86-10004
ISBN 0-8057-6936-6

Contents

About the Author
Preface
Chronology

About the Author

Mary S. Wagoner, professor of English at the University of New Orleans, received a B.A. from North Texas State University in 1953. She attended the University of Minnesota as a Woodrow Wilson Fellow and received an M.A. (1957) and a Ph.D. (1961) in eighteenth-century English literature from the University of Texas. She has taught at the University of Wyoming and, since 1963, at the University of New Orleans. Among her publications are several articles on eighteenth-century writers, a freshman textbook, and a comprehensive bibliography on Tobias Smollett.

themes in continually fresh and amusing ways. Wagoner happily manages to illuminate the brilliance of Christie's intricate story-telling without giving away the surprise endings. The result is a stimulating study sure to send new and old Christie readers out in search of more.

The Author

Mary S. Wagoner is professor of English at the University of New Orleans. A regular reviewer for *Choice,* she is also the author of a textbook for freshman English courses, a comprehensive bibliography on Tobias Smollett, and several articles on eighteenth-century British literature.

Preface

The most salient single fact about Agatha Christie is that she wrote prolifically. When she was not writing because it was her business to write, she wrote for fun.

Millions have read her work. Her detective tales in particular have become a pleasant fact of life one can find almost anywhere. Most people who let their casual reading matter accumulate seem to have at least some Christies lying about. As a resident of Picayune, Mississippi—as small a town as the name implies—I have discovered at least half of her ninety-odd books in the houses of my friends and neighbors.

Some time ago my husband and I spent a year or so renting other people's homes in Britain and on the Continent. We found some Christie novels in every house or apartment we occupied. In a city planner's house in Edinburgh, her novels competed for shelf space with awesome technical books. A cottage in Sussex belonging to a professional translator contained a truly impressive assortment of Christies in every modern European language. A closet in an apartment in a little town south of Genoa held fewer volumes, but there were a dozen or so in Italian.

These limited personal experiences only illustrate a fact to which Agatha Christie's stunning sales records attest: reading her whodunits has been an international pastime for decades.

While many have read Agatha Christie's detective novels and stories and her thrillers, and many have seen her plays, there are Christie works that have had much smaller audiences: her straight novels, her two autobiographical books, her verse, and her book for children.

Confronting the sheer bulk of Christie's published work, one attempting to review her whole career faces several special problems, the greatest of which is the number of Christie titles. One must choose between selecting samples of her work from the various genres or giving passing notice to all her writings. Since Christie specialized in surprise endings, one must also decide whether or not to honor the custom of not revealing these endings. Then, granting that explaining the Christie phenomenon has become a growth industry, one must determine how deeply to dip into the literary, sociological, and psychological theorizing her works have generated.

I have elected to comment, however briefly, on the bulk of the Christie canon. That I have failed to locate a printed version of only one play, *Fiddlers Three,* probably says something significant about the accessibility of her writings.

I have chosen not to reveal, at least not in detail, her surprise endings. To do so, I believe, rather spoils the fun for any reader who has Christies to go. As a reader, I have yet to find an analysis of her methods that gives away endings sufficiently rewarding to justify having my reading fun spoiled.

My own tastes provided an easy answer to the question of surprise endings. The issue of extensive secondary sources was more difficult. For the purposes of this review I have cited comments that happen to interest me, but have made no effort to indicate the range of Christie studies or theories about the appeal of her works, especially of her whodunits. Further, I have chosen to omit most of my own theorizing about such matters. I am convinced that people read her stories and novels or see her plays simply because she was, nearly always, a master storyteller. In the pages that follow, I note her recurring social attitudes, observe her lifelong flirtation with supernaturalism, and remark on traces of literary influences in her works only when I feel that such considerations bear directly on the real secret of Agatha Christie's appeal, namely, her extraordinary gift for managing formulas and for keeping these formulas fresh no matter how many times she redeployed them.

Not all of Agatha Christie's writing, of course, was formulaic. Her work displays a fascinating amalgam of set patterns and highly individualized ideas. Generally speaking, however, the Christie canon shows four different kinds of writing merging in various combinations: craftsmanlike management of formulas, essentially romantic treatment of fairy-tale motifs, occasional touches of supernaturalism, and humorous analyses of manners. The following pages trace these combinations through over a half century of her work.

Further, I have knowingly violated a standing academic rule. I have not tried to quote from first editions or even from hardback editions, unless they were readily available. Most of us, I suspect, read our Christie in paperback or in public library copies. When I quote from Christie works, I quote from whatever I could most easily find on friends' bookshelves or in public libraries. Since Christie's works are available in so many various editions, the bibliography lists only the original date of publication for each.

To the particular friends most generously sharing their Christie collections, Carolyn Beech and Trudy Olive, my thanks. I am also grateful to Evelyn Chandler, Interlibrary Loan Librarian at the Earl K. Long Library of the University of New Orleans, for her help in securing other materials.

Mary S. Wagoner

University of New Orleans

Chronology

1947 *The Labors of Hercules.*

1948 *Taken at the Flood. Witness for the Prosecution and Other Stories.*

1949 Rosalind Christie Prichard marries Anthony Hicks.

1950 *The Mousetrap and Other Stories. A Murder Is Announced.*

1952 *The Mousetrap* (play). *Witness for the Prosecution* (play).

1956 Agatha Christie named Commander of the British Empire.

1958 *Ordeal by Innocence.*

1961 *The Pale Horse.*

1965 *At Bertram's Hotel.*

1967 *Endless Night.*

1969 *Hallowe'en Party.*

1970 *Passenger to Frankfurt: An Extravaganza.*

1971 Agatha Christie named Dame of the British Empire.

1972 *Elephants Can Remember.*

1975 *Curtain.*

1976 Agatha Christie dies 12 January. *Sleeping Murder.*

1977 *An Autobiography.*

Chapter One
The Life of Agatha Christie

On first look, the reticent, humorous, sensitive, upper-middle-class person with a firmly Victorian upbringing that Agatha Christie describes in *An Autobiography* seems an unlikely candidate for the title Duchess of Death. On reflection, however, she appears to have had precisely the right background, experience, tastes, and talents for one whose name serves as the generic label for classic British detective fiction.

The neat fit between Agatha Christie's life and the nature of her form must, in part, be something on the order of self-fulfilling prophecy. First, more than any other single writer, she created the shape of classic detective fiction. The methods she used and the interests she exhibited became part of what readers expect from such writing. Second, *An Autobiography* remains our best source of information about the woman who created the fiction. But in writing about herself, she clearly recognized that those who might read about her as a person would probably do so because they had read her fiction. She obviously tailored her account of herself for Christiephiles and focused on the kinds of information such readers could relate to her fiction. Her own sense of audience must inevitably have tightened the fit between her books and her life.

Born in Torquay—on 15 September 1890—Agatha Mary Clarissa Miller was the third child of American-born Frederick Alvah Miller and English-born Clarissa Margaret Beochmer Miller.[1] She spent her childhood in a fairly affluent, orderly household. With a sister and brother old enough to be away at school during her early life, she was, for practical purposes, an only child indulged by an agreeable, somewhat insouciant father, directed by an unconventional but sensitive mother, and steadied by a reassuring "Nursie." She was also blessed with two interestingly eccentric grandmothers. Further, her parents enjoyed entertaining, and though the children of the family would hardly have attended their parties, their guest list included literary figures, most notably Henry James and Rudyard Kipling.

Protective as her family circle seems to have been, the child Agatha was surrounded by people who assumed she needed to confront duties, disappointments, and her own limitations. Toward the end of her life, she unhesitatingly characterized her parents' views as Victorian, remarking that " 'to be a little lady' was well rammed home in these times." She observed that being a lady started with courtesy to dependents and "went on to such things as: 'Always leave something on your plate for Lady Manners.' 'Never drink with your mouth full.' 'Remember never to put two halfpenny stamps on a letter unless it is a bill to a tradesman.' And, of course, 'Put on clean underclothes when you are going on a railway journey in case there should be an accident.' "[2]

While the mature Agatha Christie could look back with amusement at these lessons, they surface in the detective-fiction writer's confident assumptions that society's rules must be the basis for civilized life and that little details about people's behavior reveal their fundamental characters.

Classic detective fiction, by definition, presupposes the individual's duty to exercise self-control and to accept responsibility for actions. The writer's anecdotes about her upbringing suggest that she never needed to assume this view for literary purposes. She grew up with it. She epitomized her family's view of proper reaction to disappointment, particularly the need for self-control, in a vignette about the disappearance of a pet canary. The bird was found again after young Agatha had spent a day in tears, and her mother "improved the occasion after the fashion of the time. 'You see,' she said, 'how silly you have been? what a *waste* all that crying was? *Never* cry about things until you are sure' " (*AA,* 14).

Classic detective fiction also entails character typing, the assumption that individuals run true to form and thus that their behavior falls into predictable patterns, with past actions and attitudes clues to their natures. This is a view of human nature bred into young Agatha. The Miller family had no qualms about classifying their children in such a way, and the adult Agatha Christie approved of their approach. "I think late Victorian parents were more realistic and had really more consideration for their children and for what would make a happy and successful life for them. . . . The Victorians looked dispassionately at their offspring and made up their minds about their capacities. . . . Sometimes, of course, they were wrong, but on the whole it worked" (*AA,* 33).

Agatha herself was the slow one in her family's view, but as an adult she surmised that she was slow only in comparison with an exceptionally quick mother and sister. She further suspected that her problems with being inarticulate eventually made a writer of her.

Other circumstances of her childhood may have helped too. Often left free to amuse herself with elaborately imagined companions, she invented long sequences of adventures for them. Her first fancied group were the Kittens. Then she entertained herself with a Mrs. Green who had a hundred children. Later there were the Girls. These, she remembered, stayed with her for many years, and she changed their characters as she matured. "They participated in music, acted in opera, were given parts in plays and musical comedies. Even when I was grown up I spared them a thought now and then, and allocated them the various dresses in my wardrobe" (*AA*, 86). Even when elderly, she would remark: "Oh well, I suppose it is just the same as when I was four years old talking to the Kittens. I am still talking to the Kittens, in fact?" (*AA*, 427).

Early and virtually unrestricted reading undoubtedly also helped make Agatha Christie a writer. Despite her mother's having embraced the notion that reading at a young age was bad for a child's eyes, Agatha learned to read before she was five and remembered hearing her nurse apologize about it to her mother. "I'm afraid, ma'am . . . Miss Agatha can *read*" (*AA*, 13). When her father learned that she could read, he undertook teaching her to write and introduced her to arithmetic. Then her sister, returning "finished" from Paris, tried in a desultory way to teach her French.

Like many children of her time and class, Agatha Miller was not sent to school. In fact she had no regular governess, though she did have, as a companion-teacher, a young Frenchwoman, engaged during family travels abroad, who stayed with the Millers at least three years after they returned to England.

This sort of training, with a brief interval of dancing school, is all the formal education Agatha Christie remembered before her father's death when she was eleven. The fact seems to have made her occasionally uneasy, but throughout her life she remained sceptical about schooling and inclined to believe that giving children free access to shelves full of children's books might be the best way to educate them.

As far as she was concerned, her childhood exposure to certain kinds of attitudes was more useful to her than any specific information others had tried to impart. Inclined to assert that she was never educated at all, she repeatedly insisted that her own best training had come in her early encounter with Victorian attitudes.

As the general atmosphere of her childhood equipped her with an approach to human nature that lent itself to her detective fiction, her social experiences during adolescence gave her the stuff with which she fleshed out her whodunits.

Frederick Miller had not managed his money well, and when he died, his widow had to handle expenses more carefully than before. She was determined, however, to provide Agatha with educational and social opportunities comparable to those her two older children had enjoyed. She sent Agatha to a series of schools in France to study music; she saw to it that her daughter was invited to numerous house parties; she arranged a season in Cairo in lieu of a more expensive coming-out in London; and she encouraged her reading, playgoing, and writing.

The formal schooling in France left few readily identifiable traces in her writing. She rarely used French characters or settings or musicians in her stories, and her Belgian detective, Hercule Poirot, always spoke limited, and sometimes fractured, French. Yet the French experience shaped her life in that it left her looking for alternatives to the practice of music on which her schooling in France focused. While at school she had developed ambitions to be either a concert pianist or a singer. Still in Paris she discovered that she was unable to control her tensions well enough to perform before others on the piano. Shortly after she returned to England, a family friend who sang professionally warned her that her voice would never be strong enough for opera. Her recognition that she would never "do something in music" came just as she had begun to write. Writing at that stage of her life, she later remembered, hardly did more than take the place of "embroidering cushion covers or pictures taken from Dresden china painting" (*AA*, 186). Nonetheless, had she suffered less anxiety about audiences or had her voice been stronger, young Agatha Miller might have deprived detective fiction readers of one of their major sources of entertainment.

The experience of formative adolescent years as a student in a foreign country may have had another important effect on her writing. It may have helped her learn to look more alertly at people's mannerisms than she might have done surrounded by friends and acquaintances so like herself that she took them for granted.

Her season in Cairo was meant to be a training session in social behavior. Yet that season also exposed Agatha to the Near East, and if her interest flowered only after her marriage to Max Mallowan, her first effort at novel writing was set in Egypt, and she used Egyptian and Mesopotamian settings for several stories and novels.

Her attendance at country house parties when she returned to England was even more direct training for the future writer of detective fiction. Plunged into a social situation she would use often in her tales, Agatha stored up amused observations of upper-middle-class English social oddities and eccentricities. Her skill in drawing these would later attract and hold her readers, who enjoy her mildly humorous character sketches at least as much as her neat riddle solving.

Reading habits were also a particularly important formative influence at this period of Agatha Christie's life. She recalled reading Dumas and Jules Verne shortly after her father's death, along with a batch of books for girls that her mother thought vulgar. Perhaps hoping to redirect her tastes, her mother joined with Agatha in reading Sir Walter Scott, Dickens, and Thackeray, and both her mother and her grandmother took her regularly to see theatrical performances, especially musical comedy. No Christie reader should be at a loss to see the significant influence of such experiences. Her fiction clearly belongs in the tradition of the nineteenth-century novel of manners, and her enthusiasm for theater manifests itself in her novelistic techniques as well as in her dramatic work.

Perhaps the most revealing point in Agatha Christie's review of her growing up is a matter she records but does not analyze, namely, her willingness to try her hand at composing or writing—at whatever activity she enjoyed as a member of an audience. Shortly after her sister's return from France, Agatha composed a saga about the noble Lady Madge and the bloody Lady Agatha, which the girls performed for their parents. When Agatha was eleven, a local newspaper published one of her poems, one that dealt with trams. Later she "invented" an operetta called "Marjorie" and "had a feeling I might like to write a novel called 'Agnes.' " (*AA*, 138). When she was seventeen or eighteen, the *Poetry Review* published a few of her poems. Possibly because her sister had written and published a few short stories, her mother proposed that Agatha write one to cope with the boredom during convalescence from influenza. After writing several short stories, which she later described as excessively derivative, Agatha tried writing a novel set in Cairo, called *Snow upon the Desert*.

A friend of the family, the writer Eden Phillpots, kindly read her effort and offered "very good advice."

Some of these things that you have written . . . are capital. You have a great feeling for dialogue. You should stick to gay natural dialogue. Try and cut all moralizations out of your novels; you are much too fond of them, and nothing is more boring to read. Try and leave your characters *alone* so that they can speak for *themselves* instead of always rushing in to tell them what they ought to say, or to explain to the reader what they mean by what they are saying. That is for the reader to judge for himself. You have two plots here, rather than one, but that is a beginner's fault; you soon won't want to waste plots in such a spendfree way. I am sending you a letter to my own literary agent, Hughes Massie. He will criticize this for you and tell you what chances it has of being accepted. I am afraid it is not easy to get a first novel accepted, so you mustn't be disappointed. I should like to recommend you a course of reading which I think you will find helpful. Read De Quincey's *Confessions of an Opium Eater*—this will increase your vocabulary enormously—he uses some very interesting words. Read *The Story of My Life* by Jeffreys, for descriptions and a feeling for nature. (*AA*, 183–84)

The agent Hughes Massie read her manuscript but reported that he could not place it and advised her to start another novel. Instead she wrote more poems and short stories, most of which were also rejected by publishers.

Flirtations and "two narrow escapes" from getting married diverted her, for an interval, from writing. But at this period of her life, in a discussion of Conan Doyle's stories and a French detective story called *The Mystery of the Yellow Room,* her sister Madge remarked that detective fiction would be too difficult for Agatha to write. She recalled: "From that moment I was fired by the determination that I would write a detective story. It didn't go further than that. I didn't start to write it then, or plan it out; the seed had been sown. At the back of my mind, where the stories of the books I am going to write take their place long before the germination of the seed occurs, the idea had been planted: *some day I would write a detective story*" (*AA*, 198).

In the meantime, she met Archibald Christie, a junior officer in the Flying Corps about to begin his flight training. Soon engaged, but postponing marriage for nearly two years until after World War I had begun, the couple were drawn to each other, she later believed, because they were "poles apart in . . . reactions to things" (*AA*,

202). They spent little time together during their engagement since Archie got only infrequent leaves after the war began and Agatha had become involved in first aid and home nursing classes and was then assigned to a hospital in Torquay as a Voluntary Aid Detachment (V.A.D.) nurse.

Three days before Christmas in 1914, Archie got leave and Agatha and her mother met him in London. Mrs. Miller returned to Devon, and the young couple paid a visit to Archie's mother in Clifton. On Christmas Eve they were married by special license in the parish church at Clifton, with two friends of the Christie family as the only witnesses. After Christmas Day with Mrs. Miller at Torquay, the couple left for London, where the bride saw her new husband off to France for another six months' service. She returned to Torquay to live with her mother and to resume her work at the hospital, first in the surgical ward and then in the dispensary.

In 1916, during a short leave from hospital duties, Agatha took up her sister's challenge about writing detective stories. In two weeks she almost finished *The Mysterious Affair at Styles,* for which she invented a strange-looking little Belgian detective, M. Hercule Poirot, the character who would serve her better than any other for the next sixty years. After rewriting the story to eliminate an "over complicated middle" and determining that the love interest she had originally developed was intrusive, suitable only for compact, or even forced, treatment at the end of the novel, she had the manuscript typed and began sending it to publishers (*AA,* 245–46). At least four, perhaps five, publishing houses rejected it before she sent it to the Bodley Head, John Lane. Hearing nothing from them, Agatha forgot about the manuscript entirely when her husband was posted back to England and she had to get busy finding and organizing a London flat.

Then she discovered that she was pregnant, and it was only after her daughter Rosalind was born that she heard from John Lane. To Agatha's considerable surprise, she was informed that her work would be published and was offered a contract for her next five novels.

At this stage of her life, preoccupied with her husband and child, Agatha Christie had no thought of becoming a professional writer. But when she received £50 for newspaper rights to her first book, her husband proposed that a second novel might be even more profitable. She wrote a thriller, *The Secret Adversary,* and again John Lane accepted her work and the *Weekly Times* bought newspaper rights. Then, basing her story thread on a recent highly publicized murder case in France, she wrote a third novel, *Murder on the Links*.

Agatha instantly shelved her writing when her husband accepted a position as a representative of the Empire Exposition, and for eighteen months the Christies toured the empire, promoting the exposition. When they returned to England, with Christie looking for a new job, Agatha managed to write *The Mystery of the Mill House* (later retitled *The Man in the Brown Suit*) despite the problems of settling into new quarters and fending off the determined efforts of her daughter's nurse to interrupt her writing. In 1924 she also published a collection of Poirot short stories called *Poirot Investigates*.

Recognizing that her initial contract with John Lane was a poor one from an author's point of view, Agatha began to look for a literary agent and a new publisher. She found the latter in William Collins, Sons, a firm that would henceforth publish all of her work in Britain.

It seems that Agatha was just now realizing that her work really could earn money. She reports being astonished by an offer of £500 for the serial rights to *The Man in the Brown Suit* and, following her husband's advice, bought a car with this unexpected bonanza (*AA*, 306–7).

In *An Autobiography*, Agatha recalled her attitude toward earning money from her writing. "It was by now just beginning to dawn on me that perhaps I *might* be a writer by profession. I was not sure of it yet" (*AA*, 232). Though she would, in 1925, publish *The Secret of Chimneys* and, in 1926, *The Murder of Roger Ackroyd*, she remembered these years as those in which, instead of pouring her energies into writing, she amused herself by taking lessons in sculpture, by composing a few songs "by way of vanity," and by writing a "gloomy play, mainly about incest, and a historical play about Akhnaton and Egypt (*AA*, 323).

The Murder of Roger Ackroyd not only sold better than anything she had written before, but it also enjoyed a certain notoriety, for a noisy public debate erupted over whether or not she had cheated in the identity of her murderer. Dorothy L. Sayers, among others, came to her defense, calling the ending fair.

To indulge Archie Christie's passion for golf, the couple bought a house near the links and called it Styles after her first novel. From appearances, the Christies' lives were entirely in working order. But by the end of the year, Agatha Christie's mother had died, Archie Christie was interested in another woman, and he had informed his wife of the fact while she was trying to settle her mother's affairs. The pressures were too much. On 6 December, 1926, national newspapers carried headlines about her disappearance. Her car, with pieces of her clothing in it, was found abandoned near a place called Silent Pool, near Guilford. Some 15,000 people joined in a search for her, and the *Daily News* offered £100 for information on her whereabouts. Eleven days after the disappearance, Agatha Christie was recognized at the Harrogate Hydropathic Hotel where she had registered as Teresa Neele. (Nancy Neele was the name of the woman with whom Archie Christie was infatuated and whom he later married.) Her family and doctors insisted that she was, throughout the episode, a victim of amnesia. Yet puzzling details kept surfacing. For example, on 11 December, she inserted an announcement in the *Times:* "Friends and relatives of Teresa Neele, late of South Africa, please communicate— Write Box R 702, *The Times,* E. C. 4." But she had also written a letter of inquiry about a diamond ring she had lost at Harrod's a week earlier, asking that it be forwarded to Mrs. Teresa Neele at the hotel at Harrogate. This letter raised questions because there was little doubt of her knowing that she was Agatha Christie when she lost the ring. Further, the press reported three letters addressed to Colonel Christie, Captain Campbell Christie, and Miss Charlotte Fisher, her secretary, and a police official's daughter later reported a fourth letter to the police, all from a woman signing herself Agatha Christie and reporting that she feared for her life.[3]

When she was recognized at Harrogate, the press hinted that the whole business was a publicity stunt, despite the family's explanations of amnesia. One biographer, Gwen Robyns, insists that the publicity theory in no way accords with the shy writer's personality or habits of conduct. Ms. Robyns argues that while the amnesia theory is unconvincing, the disappearance is entirely understandable if one considers Agatha Christie's desperation over her marriage. She simply chose to disappear for an interval. Perhaps she wanted to frighten Archie Christie. Perhaps she left home in a suicidal mood and went to Harrogate to think about matters. Apparently she neither anticipated nor knew how to handle the harsh glare of newspaper attention directed at her personal life.[4] Another biographer, Janet Morgan, tentatively accepts the explanation of selective amnesia and suggests that the writer worried for years about this blank in her

memory.[5] Both biographers propose that she used her Mary Westmacott novels to plumb, in fiction, the emotional trauma of her fractured first marriage.

Whatever prompted the disappearance, the Christies' marriage was
effectively over. While the couple lived apart, Agatha Christie published, in 1927, *The Big Four* and, within the year, *The Mystery of the
Blue Train,* a novel she forced herself to write while she and her
daughter were staying in the Canary Islands. In *An Autobiography* she
explains the significance of this novel for her professional career.

I was driven desperately on by the desire, indeed the necessity, to write another book and make some money.

That was the moment when I changed from an amateur to a professional.
I assumed the burden of a profession, which is to write even when you don't
want to, don't much like what you are writing, and aren't writing particularly well. I have always hated *The Mystery of the Blue Train,* but I got it
written, and sent off to the publishers. It sold just as well as my last book
had done. So I had to content myself with that—though I cannot say I have
ever been proud of it. (*AA,* 344)

If the divorce first forced Agatha Christie to accept the burden of
professionalism, perhaps it also pushed her toward stronger, maturer
fiction. From the 1930s onward she discarded the silly adolescent
chatter of her early romance thrillers, increasingly dispensed with glib
love story endings, and began to handle convincingly a wider range
of human tensions. As she discovered a new life for herself, she also
picked up new settings for her novels.

In 1928, after the divorce was final and with her daughter in
school, Agatha felt free to travel again. Although intending to visit
the West Indies and Jamaica, she changed her mind when friends advised her to see the Near East and travel by the Orient Express.

In Baghdad and again in Damascus she found it necessary to dodge
well-meaning new acquaintances who wanted to chaperone her visit.
On impulse, she decided to visit Ur, the site of an archaeological dig
supervised by Leonard Woolley.

The next summer she lent a house she owned in London to Woolley and his wife, and they invited her back to Ur for a second visit.
When she arrived, Woolley's assistant, Max Mallowan, was assigned
to escort her about. In his *Memoirs* Sir Max would reminisce: "Katherine Woolley in her imperious way ordered me to take her [Agatha
Christie] on a round trip to Baghdad and see something of the desert

and places of interest on the journey. Agatha was nervous at this request and afraid that it might cause me displeasure when I might be
looking forward to journeying home on my own. However, I found
her immediately a most agreeable person and the prospect pleasing."[6]

Agatha Christie found Max Mallowan agreeable too, and on 11
September, 1930, they were married in Edinburgh. She was fourteen
years his senior; he was Roman Catholic and she was Anglican. He
was convinced that they should marry; she was worried, needlessly it
turned out, about the age difference and about her daughter's reaction. The archaeologist persuaded the writer, and the Mallowans
shared a notably successful marriage for over forty-five years.

After their marriage, the Mallowans moved back and forth between
England and his various digs in Syria and Iraq, but her capacities for
producing volumes of detective stories increased rather than dimin-
ished as her interests expanded to include her husband's work. She
began hitting the pace of two or three books a year, a pace she would
maintain for decades.

Late in life she viewed the years between 1930 and 1938 as "particularly satisfying because they were so free of outside shadows." She
recalled, "I wrote detective stories, Max wrote archeological books,
reports and articles. We were busy but we were not under intense
strain" (*AA*, 452). But she also noted that her own writing "was now
becoming more professional and therefore a great deal less enthusias-
tic" (*AA*, 456). She began producing occasional straight novels,
signed Mary Westmacott, in addition to her detective stories, and she
started adapting her own earlier stories for the stage. As she explained
her play writing:

At that moment writing plays seemed to me entrancing, simply because it
wasn't my job, because I hadn't got the feeling that I *had* to think of a
play—I only had to write the play that I was already thinking of. Plays are
much easier to *write* than books, because you can *see* them in your mind's eye,
you are not hampered with all that description which clogs you so terribly in
a book and stops you getting on with what's happening. The circumscribed
limits of the stage simplify things for you. . . . You have only what can be
seen and heard and done to deal with. Looking and listening and feeling is
what you have to deal with. (*AA*, 459)

When World War II began for England, particularly after Professor Mallowan entered the Air Force, the Mallowans' lives changed.
Rosalind Christie married a young major, Hubert Prichard, and Aga-

tha Christie began working in a hospital dispensary again, writing to fill time while her family was away. She even experimented with writing two books at once, on the theory that if one went stale, the other might keep going.

In September 1943, Rosalind Christie Prichard gave birth to a son, Mathew, a child on whom his grandmother frankly doted. Hubert Prichard saw his son only once before being killed in action, and *An Autobiography* suggests that her daughter's situation grieved and troubled the writer deeply, perhaps as deeply as any other single event of her life.

On the whole, the war years were for Agatha Christie "a nightmare in which reality stopped" (*AA*, 495). She kept writing detective fiction, which was remarkably popular during the war years. In fact, she wrote fifteen books as Agatha Christie between 1939 and 1945, including two meant to be published posthumously: *Curtain*, a Poirot novel for her husband (which was actually published in 1975, just before her death), and *Sleeping Murder*, a Miss Marple novel for her daughter. While Christie is cryptic in her autobiography about her detective fiction from the war years, she writes at some length about two books that did not carry the name Agatha Christie: *Absent in the Spring*, a Mary Westmacott novel, and *Come, Tell Me How You Live*, which she published as Agatha Christie Mallowan. She called writing *Absent in the Spring* "an imperative" and explained that she felt a special affection for *Come, Tell Me How You Live* because it was written out of nostalgia for Max Mallowan while he was stationed in North Africa (*AA*, 486).

When she and Professor Mallowan began reconstructing their private lives and careers after the war, her work pace slackened for a short period. Then both Mallowans began highly successful work that led to one major honor after another.

For his archaeological discoveries at Nimrud, Professor Mallowan was named Fellow of Old Souls, Oxford, Professor Emeritus of Western Asiatic Archaeology at the University of London, and trustee of the British Museum. He was also named Commander of the British Empire in 1960 and was knighted in 1968.

His wife had some share in his career: she accompanied him on his digs and helped photograph and catalogue his finds. But her own career also flourished. Between 1946 and 1976, the year of her death, as Agatha Christie she published thirty-eight novels and collections of short stories, one children's book, and one volume of poems. As

Mary Westmacott she published three more novels, and she wrote the autobiography that was published after her death. Further, she became an extremely active dramatist.

Her name had been on marquees before. But excepting *Black Coffee* (1930), the early plays bearing her name were others' adaptations of her short stories or novels. The first novel she adapted herself was the 1943 *Ten Little Niggers* (or *Ten Little Indians*). Other plays followed quickly: *Appointment with Death* in 1945, *Murder on the Nile* in 1946, and *Murder at the Vicarage* in 1949. In 1951, *The Hollow* opened, and within the year so did *The Mousetrap*, the play that now holds the record for a continuous run of over thirty years. After *The Mousetrap*, Agatha wrote or adapted ten other plays, including the especially popular 1953 *Witness for the Prosecution* and the 1954 *Spider's Web*, but none has equaled the staying power of *The Mousetrap*.

Further, a number of her plays and novels have been adapted for movies and television. But she did not herself participate in these adaptations and reputedly disliked the films she saw except for the E.M.I. Productions version of *Murder on the Orient Express*. Not even her great admiration for Margaret Rutherford persuaded her that Rutherford's Miss Marple films were close enough to the Marple books.[7]

Though enjoying record-setting sales of her work as well as popular acclaim, Agatha Christie found herself in a bizarre financial situation during the postwar decades. The United States Internal Revenue Service tied up her very considerable earnings from American sales even as the British Inland Revenue Service tried to collect taxes on income the writer had not, in fact, received. By 1948 her agents were scrambling so that she could avoid bankruptcy, and negotiations over the tax situations went on until the late 1960s.[8]

Happily, Agatha Christie had several peaceful years after the tax problems were solved, and in addition to a continually rising demand for her fiction in particular, she enjoyed public honors similar to those accorded Max Mallowan. Queen Elizabeth presented her with the C.B.E. in 1956, and in 1971 she was named Dame of the British Empire.

Her energy remained high until very near the end of her life, that is, until the summer of 1971, when she fell and broke a hip while in London negotiating publication of her eighty-first novel, *Nemesis*. She mended, but her strength never fully returned.

By 1975 her health was failing, and she died on 12 January, 1976.

She was buried in St. Mary's churchyard, Cholsey, Berkshire, a churchyard she had chosen ten years before. Her tombstone records her
name, her age, the phrase "Agatha Christie the writer," and an in-
scription from Spenser's *The Faerie Queene:*

> Sleep after toil
> Port after stormie sea,
> Ease after warre,
> Death after life,
> Does greatly please.

Chapter Two
Short Stories

In *An Autobiography* Agatha Christie reports rereading her first short story, the one she had written at the age of eighteen while convalescing from influenza.[1] As an experienced professional writer she found flaws in the story. She thought it a little precious, a little too much influenced by D. H. Lawrence. Yet, she declared, it did show promise (*AA,* 181).

During the course of her career, Agatha Christie published at least 149 short stories, but she did most of her work in this form in the 1920s and 1930s. Her stories usually appeared first in magazines, and 147 have been published—some repeatedly and some with variant titles—in twenty-one separate British and American collections.[2] Though many stories in the later collections were written twenty to thirty years before they were anthologized, the collections offer the only practical basis for reviewing her short fiction.

In content, Agatha Christie's short stories fall into four categories: straight tales of detection, tales with occult or supernatural elements, stories mixing a little detection with romance, and stories mixing detection with wry definition of single character types.

Regardless of category, the Christie short story preserves an essentially nineteeth-century flavor. The writer makes plot the critical element, and she always invents end-directed plots. She sets up situations that center on puzzles of one kind or another and moves efficiently toward closure of any questions she has raised, that is, toward a resolution offering a surprising explanation of the cause of the situation rather than an open-ended indication of its effects. Virtually all of her resolutions involve sudden twists. They explain why things have happened, and they assert simply, sometimes simplistically, that there are intelligible explanations for events.

The answer to the puzzle in a Christie short story generally surprises by *being* an answer. In her novels, the writer usually plays with elaborate misdirection. In her stories, by contrast, the fact of an answer frequently surprises enough.

No single Christie story represents her strength or variety, but in order to see how she worked in the form, let us consider the ending of one of her early stories, "Tragedy at Marsdon Manor" from the 1924 *Poirot Investigates*. This story illustrates the kind of structure she used for most of her stories throughout her career.

The writer sets up a mystery as Hercule Poirot explains to his friend Hastings that he has been asked by an insurance company to investigate a death. (Did a heavily insured man with financial problems die of internal hemorrhage as a doctor found, or did he, in some way, commit suicide?) She fills in details that raise questions about events. (The doctor, who believed the dead man to have been a Christian Scientist, performed no autopsy; the widow, who reports that her husband had been gravely concerned about his health, is clearly distressed when a striking young man whom she believed to be journeying to East Africa interrupts a visit from Poirot and Hastings.) Next she provides complicating hocus-pocus. (As Poirot and Hastings visit the widow, she thinks she sees her husband's ghost and hears him tapping at the window.) Then she offers reasonable explanations for the hocus-pocus. (After the widow confesses to the murder of her husband, Poirot introduces the actor who had impersonated the dead man and the policeman who had tapped on the widow.) Finally she accounts for Poirot's suspecting the widow (he noticed rouge on her eyelids) and lets Poirot tie up loose ends. (Since no one could have pulled the trigger of a rifle while holding its barrel in his mouth, logic insists that the widow must have asked her husband to demonstrate how suicide with a rook rifle could have taken place; when her husband put the rifle barrel in his mouth, she must have pulled the trigger herself.)

In later stories, Agatha Christie often invented better puzzles and more striking character sketches, but her pattern of defining situation, supplying puzzling elaboration, and following that with rapid, startling resolution continued to serve her. Her stories rarely offer complex character analysis and involve only vestigial character development in the sense of a character's growing or changing. Nor do many of her stories provide stylistic subtleties. Though capable on occasion of arresting description, Agatha Christie focuses on *what* happens and on suspense over what can happen next rather than on inviting multilayered response to events. She appeals to different kinds of response from story to story, but any given story tends to arouse only one sort of response, a response coupled, always, with a bit of surprise.

She wrote the stories in *Poirot Investigates* for *Sketch* magazine. The British edition contains eleven stories, and the American edition three more. All feature Poirot, but in two stories from the American edition, "The Lost Mine" and "The Chocolate Box," Hastings appears only as an audience to whom the little detective recounts adventures he had conducted on his own.

Though the stories exhibit considerable surface variety, all are straight tales of detection. Twelve of those in the American edition, for example, are set in England, but Poirot moves about London neighborhoods, makes excursions to country houses, and visits Brighton. In "The Chocolate Box" the author offers the only Poirot tale set in the detective's native Belgium, and she sets "The Adventure of the Egyptian Tomb" in Egypt. In addition to changes in setting, the stories present Poirot with several kinds of cases. In six stories he identifies murderers; in three he exposes attempted fraud; in two he catches jewel thieves; and in the other three he focuses on a kidnaping, a missing will, and an affair of gang revenge.

Despite differences in the nature of the puzzles Poirot solves, eleven of the stories are of a piece in structure and in method of managing surprise. They all follow a clear three-stage formula. A client presents a problem or Hercule Poirot reports one. As the investigation begins, Hastings jumps to a set of false conclusions owing to his susceptibility to pretty women ("The Adventure of 'The Western Star,' " "The Tragedy at Marsdon Manor," "The Mystery of Hunter's Lodge," and "The Veiled Lady"), his preconceptions about social types ("The Million Dollar Bond Robbery," "The Adventure of the Egyptian Tomb," "The Kidnapped Prime Minister," and "The Adventure of the Italian Nobleman"), or his uncritical acceptance of appearances ("The Adventure of the Cheap Flat," "The Disappearance of Mr. Davenheim," and "The Jewel Robbery at the Grand Metropolitan"). Then after Hastings leads the reader into a false analysis of the case, Poirot provides surprise with a correct explanation built on attention to details that Hastings had either ignored or misinterpreted. "The Lost Mine" and "The Chocolate Box" differ from the other stories mainly in that some other character fills Hastings's customary role as stooge.

In these stories, Agatha Christie obviously recalls Arthur Conan Doyle's tales of Sherlock Holmes, but she shows some movement away from her model in Poirot's methods. Holmes generally solved his cases by observing more carefully and analyzing more thoroughly than anyone else. Poirot's successes depend on his seeing through smoke screens that fool others. Refusing to accept artfully contrived illusions, he does not outwit his adversaries as Holmes generally did; he simply manages not to be fooled by them. Detectives who would not be diverted by smoke screens became, of course, a basic element in most of Christie's work, whether in stories or in novels.

As the young writer reused the characters of Poirot and Hastings from *The Mysterious Affair at Styles* in *Poirot Investigates,* so in her second short story collection, the 1929 *Partners in Crime,* she again works with characters she had already invented for a novel, Tommy and Tuppence Beresford from the 1922 romance thriller, *The Secret Adversary.* The young adventurers (who had been about to marry at the end of the novel) work with Mr. Carter, their shadowy friend from the Secret Service, at whose request they set up a detective agency.

Though self-contained, the stories in *Partners in Crime* have an exceptionally strong connecting thread. In each separate adventure, the Beresfords play at acting and talking like various fictional detectives, and in their speech and manner Agatha Christie parodies her rivals and herself.

Not all the writers and fictive detectives are still familiar to most readers. The list includes Richard Austin Freeman's Dr. John Thorndyke ("The Affair of the Pink Pearl"), Douglas Valentine's brothers Desmond and Major Okewood ("The Adventure of the Sinister Stranger"), Isabel Ostrander's McCarty and Riordan ("Finessing the King" and "The Gentleman Dressed in Newspaper"), Arthur Conan Doyle's Sherlock Holmes and Dr. Watson ("The Case of the Missing Lady"), Clinton H. Stagg's Thornley Colton ("Blindman's Bluff"), G. K. Chesterton's Father Brown ("The Man in the Mist"), Edgar Wallace's Busies ("The Crackler"), Baroness Emma Orczy's Old Man in the Corner ("The Sunningdale Mystery"), A. E. W. Mason's Inspector Hanaud ("The House of Lurking Death"), Freeman Wills Crofts's Inspector French ("The Unbreakable Alibi"), Anthony Berkeley's Roger Sheringham ("The Clergyman's Daughter" and "The Red House"), Reggie Fortune's H. C. Bailey ("The Ambassador's Boots"), and Christie's own Hercule Poirot ("The Man Who Was No. 16").[3]

Christie keeps her parodic touch light. For instance, when Tommy plays Sherlock Holmes, Tuppence protests, "If you must be Sherlock

Holmes . . . I'll get you a nice little syringe and a bottle labelled cocaine, but for God's sake leave that violin alone."[4] Slight as detective puzzlers, the stories depend on this level of fun. In several, circumstances that appear to be crimes turn out to be mere misunderstandings, and only three of the fifteen stories involve murder.

Though the general temper of these stories differs markedly from that of the stories in *Poirot Investigates,* the two collections exhibit curiously similar mixes of situations. Each contains stories about actresses, stories about Mafia-type gangs, stories about missing pearls, stories about political figures, stories about houses whose current owners need to find hidden wills or treasure to maintain what they have inherited, stories about thieves seeking out detectives, and stories that turn on chocolate boxes. Read side by side, the two collections thus demonstrate a continuing feature of the writer's work: her tendency to reuse basic ideas clothed in new dress. With these stories, a change in detectives makes the biggest difference in the appearance of the dress.

All but two of Agatha Christie's fourteen Harley Quin stories are included in the 1930 *The Mysterious Mr. Quin,* the collection that shows her bittersweet romantic vein and her impulse to fairyland fantasy. In *An Autobiography,* the writer recalled: "These are my favorite. I wrote one, not very often, at intervals perhaps of three or four months, sometimes longer still." As his creator explained, Mr. Quin "was a kind of carryover for me from my early poems in the Harlequin and Columbine series." She added:

Mr. Quin was a figure who just entered into a story—a catalyst, no more— his mere presence affected human beings. There would be some little fact, some apparently irrelevant phrase, to point him out for what he was: a man shown in a harlequin-coloured light that fell on him through a glass window; a sudden appearance or disappearance. Always he stood for the same things: he was a friend of lovers, and connected with death. Little Mr. Satterthwaite, who was, as you might say, Mr. Quin's emissary, also became a favorite character of mine. (*AA,* 420)

Stylistically the surest and cleanest of Agatha Christie's early stories, the Quin-Satterthwaite tales use conventional detective-fiction puzzles only as a base for a mix of sentimental fantasy and customary Christie firmness about conventional moral order. All but one of the stories address either painful choices between ordinary or intense living and loving or the risk that dreams can lead either to a dream house or a rubbish heap. Several trace the effects of misunderstandings or false accusations on chances for ordinary happiness. In five of the collected stories, artists of one kind or another embody intensity. In other stories, at least one character tries to live at an uncommonly high pitch. The surprises of the stories depend in large part on shifting back and forth between resolutions that favor intensity and those that favor ordinariness.

Though Mr. Satterthwaite would appear in one novel, the 1935 *Three-Act Tragedy,* or *Murder in Three Acts,* the writer never used Harley Quin in her longer fiction. But in her next short story collection, *The Thirteen Problems,* or *The Tuesday Club Murders* (1932), she invented one of her favorite novel detectives, Miss Jane Marple.

For the collection, Agatha Christie added seven new Miss Marple stories to six she had written for magazine publication in 1928. Despite the American title, only the first six stories actually involve the six people in the Tuesday Club, four of whom she reused in the other Marple tales: Miss Marple herself, retired Sir Henry Clithering of New Scotland Yard, Miss Marple's nephew Raymond West, and West's fiancée whose name would later be changed from Joyce to Joan Lemprière. The Tuesday club includes two characters the author never used again, Dr. Pender, an elderly clergyman, and Mr. Petherick, a solicitor. Each of the group agrees to report a technically unsolved mystery to which he knows an answer, and the others compete in deducing that answer.

The second six stories follow the same format but involve new companions for Miss Marple and Sir Henry: Colonel and Mrs. Bantry (who would figure in several Miss Marple novels), the beautiful but stupid actress, Jane Helier, and a Dr. Lloyd. The thirteenth story shows Miss Marple, Sir Henry, and the Bantrys dealing with a real murder instead of reporting a mystery.

The stories are highly patterned in that Miss Marple always discovers the solution, which the teller has usually learned from the culprit's confession or which the police have discovered from his trying to repeat the crime. Placidly knitting fluffy things, Miss Marple spots the answer in "The Idol House of Astarte," "Ingots of Gold," "The Blood-Stained Pavement," and "The Blue Geranium" because she refuses to be gulled by atmosphere. In "Motive v. Opportunity" and "The Four Suspects," childhood memories guide her. In "The Tuesday Night Club," "The Thumb Mark of St. Peter," "The Blue Geranium," and to some extent in "Ingots of Gold" and "Death by

Drowning," household experience leads her to notice what others miss. In "The Tuesday Night Club," "The Blue Geranium," "The Companion," "The Four Suspects," "A Christmas Tragedy," "The Herb of Death," and "The Affair at the Bungalow," she analyzes cases accurately by seeing parallels between the personalities involved and villagers she has known. As she insists, "I always find one thing very like another in this world," and "there is a great deal of wickedness in village life."⁵

Though these bases for deduction would serve as Miss Marple's primary tools in all the thirteen novels and twenty-two short stories in which she would eventually figure, the writer makes notable changes in Miss Marple's character even within the first collection of Marple stories. In the first six stories, Miss Marple is a Victorian old lady, the target of others' mild amusement. Her shrewdness surprises her company, who notice her period-piece appearances but then almost forget her until she explains everything. In the second seven stories (written after *Murder at the Vicarage,* the first Marple novel), her companions rarely overlook her. Her views become increasingly the focus of any work in which she appears, and her analyses themselves become increasingly complex. Further, the second batch of stories, excepting the third-person "Death by Drowning," exhibit a stronger sense of narrator's voice than the first batch. It is this sense, coupled with more elaborate definition of Miss Marple's personality, that marks the direction of Agatha Christie's movement as a writer, movement toward fusion of classic detective puzzle making with sharp definition of varied character types.

The Thirteen Problems occupies an especially important niche in the Christie canon, not only because it introduces her second most popular detective, but also because the stories in the collection proved a notable source of reusable ideas. Apart from Miss Marple herself, and the associates who would crop up in many stories and novels, and apart from St. Mary Mead as a setting, the plot devices of the stories became Christie standbys. "The Blood-Stained Pavement" sets up the same kind of game with eternal triangles as "Triangle at Rhodes" in *Murder in the Mews* (1937) or *Evil under the Sun* (1941). "The Companion" develops an idea repeated in *A Murder Is Announced* (1950), and "Herb of Death," one repeated in *Postern of Fate* (1973). Additionally, "The Idol House of Astarte" involves the use of ceremony to cover facts—a gambit also used in 'The Affair of the Victory Ball," another early story, which would be anthologized in *The Under Dog* (1951).

The 1933 *Hound of Death* was published as a collection only in Britain, but the separate stories have all appeared in various American anthologies. Dennis Sanders and Len Lovallo propose that the tales may antedate *The Mysterious Affair at Styles,* that is, that they were written before 1916.[6] Certainly they indicate an interest in psychic phenomena that surfaced in her later work only in two of the Mary Westmacott novels.

Instead of a common main character, these stories share elements of supernaturalism. Except for "The Witness for the Prosecution," which was the basis for the 1953 play, all the stories turn on occult business. In "The Hound of Death" a nun can will explosions. In "The Red Signal" a young man receives extrasensory warnings of danger. In "The Fourth Man" one character's personality usurps the body of another character. "The Gipsy" is a tale about a man to whom, at times of crisis, various women look like gipsies. A particularly eerie tale, "The Lamp," deals with a child ghost who requires a playmate. "The Call of Wings" (the second story Agatha Christie wrote, according to her biographer Janet Morgan)[7] involves a quasi-Christian, quasi-pagan experience with the music of a Pan figure, and "The Last Seance" is a story about a medium destroyed by a mother's passion for a dead child. In four stories—"Wireless" (alternately titled "Where There's a Will"), "The Strange Case of Sir Arthur Carmichael," "The Mystery of the Blue Jar," and "SOS"—humans engineer the appearances of supernatural events either for nefarious purposes or as appeals for help.

The 1934 collection, *The Listerdale Mystery,* was also published only in Britain, with the separate stories later included in two American anthologies, *Witness for the Prosecution and Other Stories* (1948) and *The Golden Ball and Other Stories* (1971). The collection exhibits the optimistically romantic side of the writer. Eight of the dozen stories in *The Listerdale Mystery* are lighthearted little tales about ordinary "nice" people, mostly young, who luckily satisfy their hearts' desires. Only four stories, "Philomel Cottage," "Sing a Song of Sixpence," "Accident," and "Swan Song" involve murder. As the reviewer for the *Times Literary Supplement* (London) observed, "After a heavy meal of full-course detective stories these *friandises* melt sweetly—perhaps too sweetly—on the tongue; but they are, without exception, the work of an experienced and artful cook, whose interest it is to please."[8]

Most of the stories in Agatha Christie's other 1934 collection, *Parker Pyne Investigates,* or *Parker Pyne, Detective,* are sweet too, but a sharper sense of the flaws of human nature and more intricate plotting make them on the whole more interesting stories than those of *The Listerdale Mystery*.

The first six, written for magazine publication in 1932, are similar in flavor to the stories in *The Listerdale Mystery*. Set in England, they involve Parker Pyne's putting to rights the problems of clients who answer his advertisement: "ARE YOU HAPPY? IF NOT, CONSULT MR. PARKER PYNE." Mr. Pyne, a retired civil servant, puts his experience in working with statistics to use in determining how frustrations and anxieties can be solved. Generally, his solutions depend on his effecting a change in the unhappy client's self-esteem, and he brings about the change by throwing unhappy people into fresh situations that cause others to value them even as they learn to value themselves.

In his solutions, Pyne cynically uses assistants, two of whom hold special interest because they figure in later Christie works. Mrs. Ariadne Oliver, who would appear in seven novels as the author's self-parody, has a small part in one story and is mentioned in another. Miss Felicity Lemon, who serves as Pyne's secretary, would become Hercule Poirot's for several short stories and four novels.

The second six Parker Pyne stories are more conventional fiction than the first six in that all involve either murder or theft and all have notably ingenious plot twists. All are set in the Near East (where Agatha Christie was traveling extensively with her archaeologist husband, Max Mallowan), and four use settings the writer would employ in full-length novels. Like *Murder on the Orient Express,* "Have You Got Everything You Want?" takes place on the Orient-Simplon Express. "The Gate of Baghdad" is set in Baghdad and on the road between Damascus and Baghdad, as *Murder in Mesopotamia* and *They Came to Baghdad* would be. "The Pearl of Price" is set in Petra, which Christie would use again for *Appointment with Death,* and "Death on the Nile" shares the setting and the title, but not the plot and characters, of the later novel.

Agatha Christie's next anthology, the 1937 *Murder in the Mews,* or, less one story, *Dead Man's Mirror,* is an exceptional collection on two counts. First, "Murder in the Mews" and "Dead Man's Mirror," the tales that supplied the anthology titles, are novellas rather than short stories. The other story from both British and American editions, "Triangle at Rhodes," is at least twice as long as the typical Christie short story, and "The Incredible Theft," included only in the British edition, is not much shorter. Second, three of the stories, "Murder in the Mews," "Dead Man's Mirror," and "The Incredible Theft," are reworked, expanded versions of stories Christie had published earlier in magazines. The other story, "Triangle at Rhodes," develops a situation—a triangle that characters and, presumably, readers misinterpret—common to the 1930 *Murder at the Vicarage,* the 1937 *Death on the Nile,* and most conspicuously, the 1941 *Evil under the Sun,* very nearly an extended rewrite of the short story.

The relationships between the separate tales in the anthologies, the shorter stories on which they are based, and the longer novel developed from one of them are worth studying for those interested in Agatha Christie's methods. Without undue revelation of the surprise endings of the separate works, one can note that in expanding a plot situation, the writer gives her characters new identities, delays crimes for fuller character development, adds red herrings, finds new ways to make the same important points, and develops more bits of action and reaction in the comedy of manners vein.

For example, the difference between "Murder in the Mews" and the earlier "Market Basing Mystery" (not available in anthologies until the 1951 American collection, *The Under Dog and Other Stories,* and again in the 1974 *Poirot's Early Cases,* or *Hercule Poirot's Early Cases*) involves switches in the age and sex of the victim, differences in the relationships between the victim and the friend who wishes to protect him, and changed but comparable motives. In both tales, the writer invents circumstances to establish the important point of the victim's right-handedness or left-handedness; in both, Poirot confronts deliberately arranged false clues; and in both, the absence of cigarette smoke in a closed room leads him to ask the right questions. Examining these variations, a reader inevitably notices the distinctions between Christie's basic plot patterns and her manipulation of surface details.

"Dead Man's Mirror" exhibits a comparable relation to "The Second Gong," a story anthologized in the 1948 *Witness for the Prosecution and Other Stories.* To the basic locked room plot and least likely murderer of "The Second Gong," the writer adds in "Dead Man's Mirror" the cameo appearance of Mr. Satterthwaite of the Harley Quin stories, a larger number of eccentric characters, and a larger quantity of description and dialogue—including quotation from Tennyson, the poet Poirot quotes most heavily in the late Christie novels.

The change between "The Incredible Theft" and the 1920s magazine story, "The Submarine Plans" (available in the 1951 *Under Dog and Other Stories*) is largely a matter of updating. Instead of stolen submarine plans, "The Incredible Theft" has bomber plans. The writer also alters setting and characters' names, and most important from the point of view of structure, she delays the crime and Poirot's entrance until she has developed major characters in some detail. Between "The Triangle at Rhodes" and the later novel, *Evil under the Sun,* she makes more substantive changes. For the novel she invents a new plot resolution, though she reuses her old setting, and she draws the same kinds of relationships among principal characters, though the short story offers fewer characters and complications than the novel.

The 1939 *Regatta Mystery* was published only in the United States. All the stories had come out earlier in magazines, and all except "Yellow Iris" were eventually included in various British collections.

The Regatta Mystery contains two Parker Pyne stories ("The Regatta Mystery" and "Problem at Pollensa Bay"), five Poirot stories ("The Mystery of the Baghdad Chest," "How Does Your Garden Grow?"— which lays out the plot reused in the 1937 *Dumb Witness,* or *Poirot Loses a Client,* "Yellow Iris"—which with Colonel Race replacing Poirot would become the 1945 *Sparkling Cyanide,* or *Remembered Death,* "The Dream," and "Problem at Sea"), one Miss Marple story from *The Thirteen Problems,* and one bizarre supernatural tale without a series figure ("In a Glass Darkly"). Except "Problem at Pollensa Bay" and "In a Glass Darkly," all the stories involve crimes, and even the exceptions have plots with tricky surprise endings.

Story for story, *The Regatta Mystery* is the best of the miscellaneous Christie anthologies. It represents her range and includes some of her most effectively structured stories. "The Mystery of the Baghdad Chest," for instance, is a firmly cerebral Poirot puzzle. "Miss Marple Tells a Story," a modification of the locked room gambit, turns, as the Marple tales tend to, on the lady's not being fooled because she notices revealing mannerisms. Though Parker Pyne plays a smaller role than usual in his stories, "The Regatta Mystery" displays his sympathetic shrewdness appealingly even as it effectively sketches a group of rather vulgar nouveaux riches characters, types Christie rarely handled. Finally, in "In a Glass Darkly," the writer offers one of her better crypto-Gothic tales in the vein of Poe.

Agatha Christie's best single-figure collection, the 1947 *Labors of Hercules,* which was also her cleverest set of thematically linked stories, followed *The Regatta Mystery.* Delivered in 1939 for publication in *Strand* magazine,[9] the stories in the collection exploit Poirot's Christian name.

While Poirot's personality and references to his past extend the characterization she had created for him in earlier novels and stories, the whole series of stories in *The Labors of Hercules* represent a new experiment for the author. In her earlier set of stories held together by a literary tie, *Partners in Crime,* she had only parodied detective-fiction writers. In *The Labors of Hercules,* she engages not so much in parody of the myths of Hercules as in complex comic adaptation.

Teased by a learned friend into seeing himself as a modern Hercules—though "very distinct from that unpleasant sketch of a naked figure with bulging muscles, brandishing a club"—Poirot recognizes that the other Hercules had also been "instrumental in ridding the world of certain pests." He resolves not to follow his prototype too closely, but he imposes on himself twelve last labors to be selected because they parallel Hercules'.

Poirot's friend's ruminations on the names of his godchildren strike the prevailing note of the collection.

Blanche, one of 'em is called—dark as a gypsy! Then there's Deirdre, Deirdre of the Sorrows—she's turned out merry as a grig. As for young Patience, she might as well have been named Impatience and be done with it! And Diana—well, Diana. . . . Weighs twelve stone *now*—and she's only fifteen! They *say* it's puppy fat—but it doesn't look that way to me. *Diana*! They wanted to call her Helen, but I did put my foot down there. Knowing what her father and mother looked like! And her grandmother for that matter![10]

The whimsically reductive mockery goes on through the separate episodes as the writer wittily juxtaposes her little detective's heroism with Hercules' and modern with classical social pests. The case of "The Nemean Lion" involves the kidnapping of a lionhearted Pekinese. In "The Lernean Hydra" Poirot slays the many-headed beast, rumor. In "The Arcadian Deer" he makes a match between a mechanic and a tubercular ballet dancer with hair like wings of gold or the horns of a stricken deer. Poirot tangles with a professional gangster in "The Erymanthian Boar." In "The Augean Stables" he saves an English government leader by turning one of "the great forces of nature"—sex scandal—like a river through stables fouled by political chicanery. "The Stymphalean Birds," in contrast to other stories in the collection, presents standard Christiean misdirection about who is practicing blackmail. In "The Cretan Bull," the writer plays punning tricks while unraveling a maze of questions about inherited madness. "The Girdle of Hyppolita," another piece of typical Poirot investigation, deals with art theft and kidnapping, with a connection to the Greek myth more literal than figurative. In "The Flock of Geryon," however, Agatha Christie again achieves a witty parallel between ancient legend and the present, substituting for Geryon's flock of cattle the followers of an unscrupulous leader of a religious cult. For "The Apples of Hesperides," she again resorts to a physical object to tie her story to Hercules' adventure. The apples are emeralds on a Borgia pope's goblet, but she also makes conspicuously heavy use of coincidences to tie her story to the legend. She saves her most complicated comedy for the last labor, "The Capture of Cerberus," in which she invents wildly funny modern equivalents for Greek details. Poirot smashes a drug ring run from a nightclub called Hell, with which his old acquaintance and sentimental flame, the Countess Vera Rossakoff, has involved herself.

Of the ten stories in the next collection, the 1948 *Witness for the Prosecution and Other Stories,* nine had already been anthologized in British collections. Six, including the title story, had appeared in the 1933 *Hound of Death* and three in the 1934 *Listerdale Mystery.* The new story, "The Second Gong," is a shorter version—with a different murderer—of "Dead Man's Mirror," from the 1937 *Murder in the Mews,* or *Dead Man's Mirror.*

The 1950 collection, *Three Blind Mice and Other Stories,* was published only in the United States, though seven of the nine stories appeared in later British anthologies. Four stories feature Poirot, four Miss Marple, and one Harley Quin and Mr. Satterthwaite. Most had appeared in the 1920s in magazines.

The title story is adapted from a 1947 BBC radio play commissioned as part of the celebration of Queen Mary's birthday. In 1952, eliminating Poirot, the writer revised her material again, this time into the script for the play, *The Mousetrap.* Notable as a story that "works" with or without Poirot, "Three Blind Mice" is also a rare instance of Christie's borrowing devices from her novels for a short story. As a rule, she first tried out ideas in stories, then used them in novels. But in "Three Blind Mice" she integrates elements of the nursery rhyme motif (used previously both in stories and in novels) with plot devices she had worked up for her longer fiction, namely *The Sittaford Mystery* and *Hercule Poirot's Christmas*.

The other three Poirot stories all happen to be cases Poirot solves because he is aware of people's habits. In "Four and Twenty Black-birds," in which the nursery rhyme title is almost incidental, the detective catches an impersonator who indulges his own tastes in food instead of following his victim's eating habits. In "The Third-Floor Flat," Poirot catches a murderer who pretends not to know where to find a light switch. In "The Adventure of Johnny Waverley," he spots a kidnapper because he did not remember, as a maid would have, to sweep out the corners of an elevator. But contrary to his usual custom, Poirot warns the man to avoid future foolishness instead of turning him over to the law.

The four Miss Marple stories are more varied in nature. In "Strange Jest," Miss Marple solves no crime. Instead, remembering her childish bachelor uncle, Henry, she finds a hidden fortune for a young couple by using a device repeated in the 1954 play, *The Spider's Web.* In "The Tape-Measure Murder," Miss Marple solves a murder, but her method, attention to a small clue that others have failed to notice, smacks more of Poirot's technique than Miss Marple's usual practices. "The Case of the Perfect Maid," however, displays quintessential Marple methods. The lady springs to the defense of a servant girl (as in the 1953 *A Pocket Full of Rye*), and though she solves a burglary mystery by applying both common sense and her considerable experience with village depravity, she clinches her case by carefully collecting fingerprints. "The Case of the Caretaker" similarly shows Miss Marple practicing her distinctive style of detection. While her physician, Dr. Haydock, presents the murder case to her, presumably to keep her interested as she recuperates from influenza, she spots the killer by thinking about the patterns in his behavior.

For "The Love Detectives," one of the two Quin-Satterthwaite stories not included in *The Mysterious Mr. Quin,* Agatha Christie whips up an especially surprising reversal. She carefully twists the identity of those whom Mr. Quin wishes to protect, but her focus on the other characters' reactions to a murder mystery preserves the surprise until the last moment.

The 1951 *Under Dog and Other Stories* collects early Christie tales previously published in the United States only, though the separate titles would be included in later British anthologies. The collection represents no single theme; Hercule Poirot as detective supplies the only common feature of the nine stories.

In the title story, the longest in the collection, Poirot discovers a murderer by having his victim's widow hypnotized. Under hypnosis, the lady recalls details that justify the suspicion she had attributed to her woman's intuition. Agatha Christie used the hypnotism gimmick only for this story, but as Earl F. Bargainnier observes, the story represents a basic type of Christie mystery in that it focuses on how murder was committed rather than on who did it.[11] The writer skillfully manages reader credence in Lady Astwell, the star witness who supplies necessary information even as she arouses enough distrust to keep matters unresolved until the conclusion.

Two stories in the collection anticipate later Christie work. In "The Plymouth Express" we find an earlier, and simpler, version of the main plot of the novel, *The Mystery of the Blue Train*. "The Submarine Plans," expanded fourfold, became "The Incredible Theft." Two other stories represent early experiments in devices important in later work. We have noted the connection between "The Market Basing Mystery" and "Murder in the Mews." The device of Poirot's answering a summons only to discover that his correspondent has already been murdered, an important element of "The Cornish Mystery," had also served the writer in the 1923 *Murder on the Links* and would serve her again in the 1937 *Dumb Witness,* in "How Does Your Garden Grow?" and in "Dead Man's Mirror." "The Lemesurier Inheritance" involves the same kind of genetic puzzle Poirot solved in "The Erymanthian Boar."

The other three stories, though all adequate as short mysteries, are most memorable for their representations of certain milieus of English life in the 1920s. "The Affair of the Victory Ball," which betrays a recurring Christian interest in commedia dell'arte, has a cast of smart young things. "The King of Clubs," another case Poirot solves by noticing family resemblances, features an upper-middle-class provincial family. "The Adventure of the Clapham Cook," a tricky tale about embezzlement and fraud, describes suburban folk and their servants.

The 1960 collection of six Christie short stories, *The Adventure of the Christmas Pudding, and a Selection of Entrées,* was published only in Britain. The title story and a Miss Marple tale, "Greenshaw's Folly," appear here for the first time in an anthology. Of the four other stories, "The Under Dog" had appeared as the title story of the 1951

American collection; "The Dream" can be found in the 1939 *Regatta Mystery,* as can be a shorter version of "The Mystery of the Baghdad Chest," there titled "The Mystery of the Spanish Shawl." "Four and Twenty Blackbirds" had appeared in 1950 in *Three Blind Mice.*

In "The Adventure of the Christmas Pudding" (retitled "The Theft of the Royal Ruby" in the 1961 collection, *Double Sin*), Poirot, maneuvered into spending Christmas in a fourteenth-century English manor house, retrieves a ruby squandered away by a Near Eastern sheik and protects a wellborn but foolish young Englishwoman from an adventurer. In "Greenshaw's Folly," Miss Marple solves a problem for her nephew Raymond West. Granting its length, the story may be the most complex Christiean game, with its locked room device and an altogether dazzling variety of disguises and masquerades.

The 1961 anthology called *Double Sin and Other Stories* is another American collection of eight tales, four written in the 1920s and four in the 1950s. "Greenshaw's Folly" and "The Theft of the Royal Ruby" (titled "The Adventure of the Christmas Pudding") were included in the 1960 *Adventure of the Christmas Pudding;* "The Last Seance" was included in the 1929 *Hound of Death.*

One of five stories first anthologized here, the title story, a Poirot-Hastings narrative from 1929, traces Poirot's efforts to foil an attempted fraud by detecting a masquerade. The later stories include "Wasps' Nest," an adventure in which Poirot prevents a complex plan for revenge; "The Dressmaker's Doll," a strange little supernatural tale, without a series detective, in which a doll moves about to satisfy her demand for love; "The Double Clue," a tale of Poirot's first encounter with the Countess Vera Rossakoff, in which the lady wins the detective's lasting admiration, both for her dramatic femininity and for her capacity to lose with grace; and "Sanctuary," a touching Miss Marple story, set in Chipping Claghorn, in which a dying man claims sanctuary in a church and in which Miss Marple assists her godchild, Bunch Harmon, in protecting his child's inheritance.

Every story in the 1965 American collection, *Surprise! Surprise! A Collection of Mystery Stories with Unexpected Endings,* had already been anthologized. Of the thirteen stories, "The Arcadian Deer" was in *The Labors of Hercules;* "Witness for the Prosecution," "Where There's a Will" and "The Mystery of the Spanish Shawl" were in *Witness for the Prosecution and Other Stories;* "The Cornish Mystery" and "The Plymouth Express" were in *The Under Dog and Other Stories;* "The Case of the Distressed Lady" was in *Mr. Parker Pyne Detective;* and "The Adventures of Johnny Waverley," "The Case of the Perfect Maid," and "The Third Floor Flat" were in *Three Blind Mice and Other Stories.* "Double Sin" and "Greenshaw's Folly" were both included in the 1961 *Double Sin and Other Stories.*

According to Janet Morgan, the other 1961 collection of short stories, *Thirteen for Luck,* subtitled "A Selection of Mystery Stories for Young Readers," irritated Agatha Christie into snorting: "My books are written for adults and always have been. . . . I *hate* this silly teen-ager business."[12] All the titles in *Thirteen for Luck* had already appeared in *Poirot Investigates, The Thirteen Problems, The Mysterious Mr. Quin, The Regatta Mystery, Partners in Crime,* or *Witness for the Prosecution.*

Of the fifteen stories in the 1971 *Golden Ball and Other Stories,* eight had appeared in *The Listerdale Mystery* and five in *The Hound of Death.* The two new stories are "Magnolia Blossom" and "Next to a Dog." "Magnolia Blossom" concerns a woman torn between loyalties to the man she loves and a husband in financial difficulties. "Next to a Dog" deals with a young woman's commitment to her aging pet terrier. Both stories represent a sentimental streak in Agatha Christie.

The 1974 *Poirot's Early Cases,* or *Hercule Poirot's Early Cases,* contains eighteen stories, all of which had already been anthologized in the United States and sixteen of which had already appeared in book-length collections in Britain. "The Lost Mine," "The Chocolate Box," and "The Veiled Lady" were included in the 1925 *Poirot Investigates.* "How Does Your Garden Grow?" and "Problem at Sea" were in the 1939 *Regatta Mystery.* "The Third-Floor Flat" and "The Adventure of Johnny Waverley" had appeared in the 1950 *Three Blind Mice.* The 1961 *Double Sin* had included "Double Sin," "The Double Clue," and "Wasp's Nest." "The Market Basing Mystery," "The Lemesurier Inheritance," "The Cornish Mystery," "The King of Clubs," "The Adventure of the Clapham Cook," and "The Plymouth Express" had all been printed in 1951 in *The Under Dog.*

The posthumously published 1979 *Miss Marple's Final Cases and Two Other Stories* similarly reprints stories already included in other anthologies. It includes "The Dressmaker's Doll" and "Sanctuary" from the 1961 *Double Sin*; "Strange Jest," "The Tape-Measure Murder," "The Case of the Perfect Maid," and "The Case of the Caretaker" from the 1950 *Three Blind Mice;* and "Miss Marple Tells a Story" and "In a Glass Darkly" from the 1939 *Regatta Mystery.*

Had Agatha Christie written neither novels nor plays, she would deserve some attention as a writer of short fiction. The ease with which she reused short story ideas in novels, and the ease with which a few were adapted for the stage, point up the fact that the differences between her short tales and her other forms were minimal, functions of length or circumstances of presentation, rather than changes in approach. While she indulged more freely in play with supernaturalism in her stories than she ever did in her novels, and while her romantic mysticism was more evident there than in any novels save the Mary Westmacotts, she was the same kind of writer in both forms. Because they are longer, the novels have more complicated, more elaborate plots, with more scope for misdirection than do the stories. As H. Douglas Thomson once observed, stories "are not so suitable a medium for 'the most unlikely person' theme as novels. Instead, stories lend themselves to development by 'the most unexpected means.' "[13]

Agatha Christie's stories, above all, represent survival of the good, quick, enjoy-at-a-single-sitting mode of short story writing. Her contemporaries working on "serious" short stories explored dimensions at which her own efforts never even hint. But she preserved a significant, satisfying tradition of the story as a brief unified tale that creates a single, decisive effect.

Chapter Three
The Detective Novels: Finding the Form (1920–1929)

Agatha Christie made her most revealing single comment on writing in general, and perhaps on writing detective novels in particular, when she discussed her reluctance to criticize others' writing. "The only thing I will advance as criticism is that the writer has not taken any account of the market for his wares," she declared. "It's no good starting out by thinking one is a heaven-born genius—some people are, but very few. No, one is a tradesman—a tradesman in a good honest trade. You must learn the technical skills, and then, within that trade, you can apply your own creative ideas; but you must submit to the discipline of form" (AA, 323).

The Form of Classic Detective Fiction

For over half a century Agatha Christie practiced the trade of writing classic, or golden age, detective novels and submitted to the discipline of that rigorously patterned form. A type of British whodunit that flourished between the world wars and is, in fact, still practiced, the classic detective novel utilizes a highly formulaic structure and a predictable manner, and it satisfies particular cultural and psychological yearnings in its readers.

As W. H. Auden defined the plot line of the form, "a murder occurs; many are suspected; all but one suspect, who is the murderer, are eliminated; the murderer is arrested or dies."[1] The other rules of classic detective novels—rules covering the nature of action, of narrative movement, of thematic thrust, of characterization, and of setting—all follow from the basic plot pattern.

Classic detective fiction calls for cerebral, rather than physical, action. Typically, the murderer conducts his business out of sight, and somebody discovers the body after the fact. The principal killing merely sets up the important developments, the assessment of the many suspects and the elimination of all but one, developments which by their nature establish the dual narrative movement peculiar to the form. First the detecting figure must discover and evaluate cases against the many suspects—business that creates forward-looking, suspense-generating movement. Having fixed on the real criminal's identity, he must provide a coherent analysis of what has happened—a performance that produces a retrospective, tension-releasing movement. To put it another way, the assessment/discovery phase of the pattern shows mind at work. The analysis, or explanation, phase exhibits the results of the mind's work, its sorting the evidence, finding the truth, achieving meaning out of confusion through the act of understanding the past. Observation of one movement and anticipation of the other combine to create reader perspective.[2]

The detective figure serves as key performer in both phases, but in his assessment of suspects and discovery of the criminal he is both model thinker and competitor to the puzzle-solving reader. His competitive role, indeed, occasions the "fair play" requirement in classic detective fiction.[3] Essentially, this requirement guarantees that the reader has at least a theoretical chance at outguessing the detective. It requires that the reader be offered a reasonable number of timely clues, though the writer may arrange matters so the reader fails to recognize a clue's importance or applies it to the wrong suspects.

For the detective novelist, no job is trickier or more critical than inventing ostensibly fair misdirection—that is, preserving some connection with plausibility while making many characters suspect. As Ariadne Oliver, Christie's fictional novelist, complains in *The Pale Horse,* the procedure itself defies common sense though it must not seem to. "I really can't think how anyone ever gets away with a murder in real life. It seems to me that the moment you've done a murder the whole thing is so terribly obvious. . . . Say what you like, it's not natural for five or six people to be on the spot when B is murdered and all to have a motive for killing B—unless, that is, B is absolutely madly unpleasant and in that case nobody will mind whether he's been killed or not, and doesn't care in the least who's done it."[4]

As explicator who solves all riddles and answers all questions in the end, a necessarily less dramatic role than that of policeman who sorts through suspects, the detective must show a mind coping with events and must effect a restoration of the social order. His performance must justify classic detective fiction's basic premise that reason can triumph, that events make sense. When the detective provides an explanation of the past event, he also isolates the agent of violence, the murderer, from society, thus demonstrating that human intelligence can promote justice.

The fact that in classic detective novels the murderer must stay hidden among the other suspects until the resolution generates the form's primary rules of characterization. One key rule requires severe restriction of direct reader access to the minds of most of the characters. The reader will not be deceived if he knows too early what the murderer or any other suspect thinks, for then he can safely narrow his suspect list. Not only must the writer veil what the characters are thinking, but he must also control empathy for most of the characters if all are to be equally suspected. The writer must be wary of betraying the reader into identification with a character who later proves to be the criminal, lest the teleological thrust of the ending be compromised. The upshot of these plot-based rules is that characterization of most figures must be externalized. Their identities must be defined in speech, gesture, and other publicly observable details. Although the reason for this approach differs from that of earlier literary traditions, the practice links classic detective novels to eighteenth-and nineteenth-century novels of manners and accounts for the form's bias toward at least mildly comic figures.

The approach to character reinforces setting requirements imposed by the plot pattern of such novels. While the plot calls for several suspects, it also demands some geographical or social circumstance that closes and limits their number, that reasonably allows each suspect both opportunity and motive for killing, and that keeps all the suspects grouped until the detective can sort them out.

Hanna Chaney notes the connection between restrictive settings and classic detective fiction's affinity to the traditional novel of manners. The requirements of setting, and those of characterization, set up "a constant interplay between the customs and mores of a certain milieu and psychological and ethical realities." While the detective or investigator, even if he belongs to the milieu in question, examines behavior for clues to guilt or innocence, he takes the reader with him in an exploration of a particular society with its own colors and nuances. This exploration, often interesting for its own sake, promotes satiric puncturing of little affectations and pretenses even while a little world also functions as a microcosm of society at large. Narrative examination of the figures within a closed setting, in short, makes an issue of the connections between a society's manners and its moral imperatives. When murder breaches a society's defenses, its code of manners is challenged with evidence that it contains hidden destructive forces. The resolution, the detective's successful identification of the murderer, brings about the murderer's exclusion and affirms, at least momentarily, the soundness of fundamental social values.[5]

Other commentators, some stressing psychological elements of response, others interested in sociological appeal, have offered additional theories of detective fiction's attraction for readers.

Among those seeing the appeal of the form as fundamentally literary, Dorothy Sayers contended that classic detective fiction satisfies the requirements of Aristotelian order, that it exhibits firm beginning, middle, and end even as it stresses consistency in character and respects probability.[6] In a comparable argument, W. H. Auden, who also observed the Aristotelian elements of the form, found in it the stuff for vicarious expiation of guilt, whether one chooses to define the expiation in Christian, Freudian, or other terms.[7]

David I. Grossvogel finds the appeal of the form in avoidance of, rather than in confrontation with, the stresses of contemporary life. He contends that, in contrast to the metaphysical confrontation with perdurable mystery, such as that presented in *Oedipus the King,* classic detective fiction "does not propose to be 'real'; it proposes only, and as a game, that the mystery is located on *this side* of the unknown. It replaces the awesomeness of limits by a false beard—a mask that is only superficially menacing and can be removed in due time. It redefines mystery by counterstating it; by assuming that mystery can be overcome, it allows the reader to play at being a god with no resonance, a little as a child might be given a plastic stethoscope to play doctor."[8]

Less generic theories about the appeal of the form stress the social vision of classic detective fiction. Marxist critic Ernest Mandel, for instance, proposes that novels in the tradition represent assertion of profound social attitudes. He asserts, "The reduction of crime, if not of human problems themselves, to 'mysteries' that can be solved is symbolic of a behavioral and ideological trend typical of capitalism."[9]

Agatha Christie's Approach

Agatha Christie herself was never much given to theoretical analyses of her form, beyond remarking that when she first began writing she saw the detective story as "the story of the chase; it was also very much a story with a moral; in fact it was the old Everyman Morality Tale, the hunting down of Evil and the triumph of Good. At that time, the time of the 1914 war, the doer of evil was not a hero; the *enemy* was wicked, the hero was good; it was as crude and simple as that. We had not then begun to wallow in psychology. I was like everyone else who wrote books or read them, against the criminal and for the innocent victim" (*AA,* 424).

Yet in her work, Agatha Christie left a significant personal imprint on the classic detective novel, both because of the conventions she herself invented and because of her experiments with stretching the limits of the rules, as she increased her own technical skills. Her novels fit loosely into groups, depending on the kinds of experiments she conducted. In some periods of her career she played with problems of technique, as though testing how many ways she could reuse a particular plot device by varying characters, situations, or settings. In other periods her interest shifted to putting one type of victim in several different sorts of plots. In yet others she examined a single social or moral question through several otherwise markedly different novels.

Though her first novel, *The Mysterious Affair at Styles,* was a detective tale, young Agatha Christie split her early efforts between whodunits and romance thrillers, which, she confessed, were easier to write.

Her account of planning *The Mysterious Affair at Styles* shows as much about her initial approach to the form as does the novel itself. Consciously imitating Conan Doyle's Sherlock Holmes tales in her basic design, she looked for ways to update characters and to use information she happened to have in details of her plot. As she understood her model, her imitation would require a preternaturally brainy, vain, and somewhat eccentric detective—of something other than official status—and a narrating companion, more obtuse than any reader could be. Belgian refugees staying in Torquay gave her the idea of using a retired Belgian policeman for her Holmes figure; while tidying her room she thought of making him obsessively fastidious. For her Watson figure she hit upon a military man, invalided and back from the war. Thus she created Hercule Poirot and his friend Hastings (*AA*, 242–43). Poirot would appear in thirty-three novels and fifty-two short stories, Hastings in eight novels and twenty-six stories, though his name would be at least mentioned in most of the Poirot tales.

Through his long career—and pundits have noted that a detective who retired in 1920 would have been approximately 136 years old when his death was announced in the 1976 *Curtain*—Hercule Poirot remained the same basic character.

Agatha Christie's invention of secondary characters for *Styles* similarly set the pattern for her work in the detective novel. In *An Autobiography*, she reported that she got hints for most of her characters from observing strangers on trains. As she remembered: "Sure enough, next day, when I was sitting in a tram, I saw just what I wanted: *a man with a black beard, sitting next to an elderly lady who was chatting like a magpie.* I didn't think I'd have *her,* but I thought *he* would do admirably. Sitting a little beyond them was a large, hearty woman, talking loudly about spring bulbs. I liked the look of her too. Perhaps I could incorporate her?" (*AA*, 242). In short, she invented characters from impressions, but they were *her* inventions. Her autobiography indicates that only a handful of her characters were ever based on people she actually knew.

In working out details for *Styles,* the writer resorted, where she could, to material she happened to know something about. For example, she made the crime a poisoning since her experience with pharmacy as a V.A.D. had taught her something about poisons. But she also relied on Doyle's trick of having the detective recognize the significance of apparently minor clues that others, including the police, had overlooked. Poirot, like Holmes, pays attention to small physical details. A smashed coffee cup, a spot of candle wax on the carpet, disarranged ornaments on a mantel, and green threads caught in a door lead him to a solution no one else considers.

Though consciously developing the major narrative elements in imitation of her model, even in her first novel she worked out variations of her own, some of which she would use again and again. For instance, Conan Doyle's Watson usually merely fails to appreciate the importance of clues; clues cause Christie's Hastings to leap to false conclusions.

The differences between Sherlock Holmes and Hercule Poirot are

yet subtler. Both find rational explanations for events when others de-
spair of an explanation's existing. Christie's Poirot is special in that,
confronted with a string of possible suspects all having motive and
opportunity, he brilliantly demonstrates the guilt of the least likely,
the apparently exonerated. Further, as Stephen Knight notices,
Poirot's fussy eccentricities and unheroic manner represent a new
twist in detective figures, a redirection of the active, heroic, male ste-
reotype, a redirection evident even in his name. A Hercules who is
also something of a *poirot,* a buffoon, he practices methods that arise
"from the world of a woman's experience and understanding, at a
time when women were largely restricted to household activity. A
broken coffee-cup, a fire lit in summer, freshly planted begonias, the
need to tidy a mantelpiece: these are the sources of information."[10]

In *Styles,* as Agatha Christie modifies her Sherlock Holmes model
to fit a pattern of plot development that would serve her repeatedly,
she also devises a cast she would almost duplicate over thirty years
later in the 1952 *They Do It with Mirrors,* or *Murder with Mirrors:* a
stepmother, stepchildren, a second husband for the stepmother, and
assorted family retainers and permanent houseguests. Further, as she
would in most of her fiction, she pairs essentially caricatural types.
Apart from contrasting the slow-witted, thoroughly English Hastings
and the clever, foreign Poirot, she pits insiders, members of the Cavendish family, against outsiders, the German Jew Dr. Bauerstein and
the victim's secretary and second husband, Mr. Inglethorp. She draws
an elder and a younger brother of radically different dispositions and
matches the quality of exquisite stillness in the elder brother's wife
with the liveliness of the girl staying with the family.

Such pairing tends to underscore Agatha Christie's literary tie to
the novel-of-manners tradition, but she had yet to develop the comic
dimensions customary in such characterization. Though most of the
characters in *Styles* have tag mannerisms—the telegraphic sentences of
the housekeeper or the bossiness of the victim—the writer really invites smiles only at Hastings's thickheaded complacency or Poirot's
boasts about his little grey cells and such slightly foreign pronounce-
ments as "A little minute . . . I come," or "Ah, my friend, I am like
a giant refreshed. I run! I leap!" or "Ah, ma foi, no! . . . This time
it is an idea gigantic! Stupendous!"

While Poirot's mannered speech shows occasional straining, Agatha
Christie on the whole manages dialogue more skillfully than one

would gather from the narrative voice of Hastings. For example, an exchange between John and Mary Cavendish runs:

"Oh," she shrugged her shoulders, "if it is only village gossip that you mind!"

"But it isn't. I've had enough of the fellow hanging about. He's a Polish Jew, anyway."

"A tinge of Jewish blood is not a bad thing. It leavens the"—she looked at him—"stolid stupidity of the ordinary Englishman."

Then we hear the heavy-handed descriptive style of the narrator, Hastings. "Fire in her eyes, ice in her voice, I did not wonder that the blood rose to John's face in a crimson tide."[11]

Reminiscing in *An Autobiography* about her first novel, Agatha Christie reported rewriting an overcomplicated middle and later, at the behest of John Lane, eliminating a final trial scene. She regretted that she had not done more rewriting to minimize the love interest of the novel, remarking that this type of subplot tends to be "a terrible bore in detective stories." Yet, showing her responsiveness to reader expectation in formula fiction, she added that "at that period detective stories always had to have a love interest" (*AA*, 246).

For her second detective novel, *Murder on the Links* (1923), the writer tried a new kind of experiment. She based a detective story on a widely publicized real crime (*AA*, 267). The crime itself may have been real, but she made the affair a puzzle for Poirot and reused Hastings as a narrator. *Murder on the Links* differs from *Styles* in that its setting is technically France, albeit a France distinguishable from England only in the names of places and characters. In most respects, Poirot and Hastings are the same characters she invented for *Styles*, except that each is somewhat more economically introduced and each more aggressively displays the qualities suggested in the earlier portraits. Poirot, for instance, enters into open rivalry with the official French investigator who follows bloodhound tactics, and Hastings, only distantly attracted to pretty, auburn-haired girls in *Styles*, falls enough in love to plan marriage.

In the plot resolution of *Murder on the Links*, the writer cheats a bit more than she would in her later work. She reserves for her final pages the information that the cast includes a set of twins, and Poirot solves the problem because he remembers an earlier case in Paris, a case the reader hears about only when Hastings does.

In the 1924 *Man in the Brown Suit,* Agatha Christie tried mixing detective novel and romantic thriller formulas with a result hardly fitting either category. The extremely loose structure does, however, set up a whodunit question, and several elements of the narrative represent her experiments with ideas and techniques she later used in successful detective novels.

Her most interesting idea was the use of two narrative voices, one primarily for the romance thread, the other for the whodunit thread. With this second voice, she anticipates the tricky surprise for readers that caused some public furor over the 1926 *Murder of Roger Ackroyd.* The first voice displays the wry comic sense she had not before employed in a detective novel. For instance, when the heroine calls at Scotland Yard, she inadvertently selects the department for missing umbrellas. Confronting a supercilious police inspector, she describes a suspect. "His head was markedly brachycephalic. He will not find it so easy to alter that." Then she observes "with pleasure that Inspector Meadow's pen wavered. It was clear that he did not know how to spell brachycephalic." Neither narrator indulges in the adverb-heavy prose of Hastings, and though Christie includes occasional faces "distorted by fear" or places with atmosphere "of cruelty, of menace, of fear," she increases her use of sensory description. In her opening description of a Paris stage, for instance, "the curtain fell with a swish, hiding the reds and blues and magentas of the bizarre decor."

In *The Man in the Brown Suit,* Agatha Christie also tries another experimental touch: the self-consciously literary echo. She invents an Adam-and-Eve-in-the-Garden-of-Eden interlude, in which two characters maintain a chaste relationship while isolated on an island in the Zambezi River. This segment serves, presumably, to reinforce a simplicity-versus-sophistication motif that runs throughout the novel, but it disrupts the narrative pace and contributes little to plot resolution.

For her plot resolution, Christie tests a device she would repeat even in the Poirot tales. The criminal, himself, helps put the puzzling pieces together in a good-humored letter at the end; unlike most Christie villains, however, he escapes unpunished. Finally, the novel introduces Colonel Race, a Secret Service agent who would appear in four of her later novels.

The 1926 *Murder of Roger Ackroyd,* the first of the vintage Christies, includes witty dialogue; characters with convincing, if larger than life, personalities; and episodes fitting together in a tightly finished plot matching the five-part plot pattern Auden defined. Moreover the novel combines neat riddle solving with honestly offered, if deftly concealed, clues and a fundamentally comic English village world.

Reusing Hercule Poirot as detective, but developing an ironic narrator in place of the slow-witted Hastings, Agatha Christie offers a better puzzle than she had invented before. None of the characters in *The Murder of Roger Ackroyd,* except for Poirot himself, can automatically be dismissed as a suspect. All of the suspects are on the scene almost from the beginning, and even those with pasts have their histories disclosed by Poirot in time for the reader to consider them as suspects.

In posing her riddle, the writer makes a more limited use of physical clues than she ever had before, though she uses Poirot's interest in a few such objects—a misplaced chair, an open display table, a scrap of starched cambric, a quill, a gold band in a fish pond—for calculated misdirection. Even then, the importance of the objects lies in their pointing to the real target of Poirot's inquiry, the psychological makeup of all the characters.

It was evidently in church rather than in the study of Freud or Jung and their followers that Agatha Christie learned the kind of psychology Poirot practices. Poirot takes susceptibility to the deadly sins for granted, and the activity of his little grey cells focuses on signs of one special susceptibility: the weakness that will lead a person to murder. Detecting these signs, remarks Stephen Knight, requires neither arduous intellectualism nor professional skills. Simple, orderly observation will serve. For Knight, this quality explains much of the author's success with readers. "The low-toned formulaic language [of guilt and innocence] effectively conceals the emotive starts of real people and the sheer complexity of values and motives; it is both materialist and naively evaluative and in this way facilitates the extraordinary plots and replicates the mechanistic and simply certain view of the world held by the author and also held—perhaps uncertainly—by [her] audience."[12]

As Poirot weighs character clues as well as physical clues, so must the reader who wishes to compete with him to find the answer to the riddle. But not many readers have outpaced Poirot in his pursuit of the killer in *The Murder of Roger Ackroyd,* no doubt, in part, because the prevailing comic flavor of the narrative disarms suspicions. The ironic narrative voice of Dr. Sheppard contributes to this flavor. He ruefully reports allowing his sister Caroline to prescribe liver pills for him as though he had no medical training at all. He notes that Roger Ackroyd is "a man more impossibly like a country squire than any country squire could really be. He reminds one of the red-faced sportsmen who always appeared early in the first act of an old fashioned musical comedy. . . . Of course, Ackroyd is not really a country squire. He is an immensely successful manufacturer of (I think) wagon wheels." As he describes his sister Caroline, somebody like her "must have invented the questions on passports. The motto of the mongoose family, so Mr. Kipling tells us, is: 'Go and find out.' If Caroline ever adopts a crest, I should certainly suggest a mongoose rampant." Or as he perceives Mrs. Ackroyd: " 'I can't tell you, my dear Dr. Sheppard, the relief to a mother's heart.' Mrs. Ackroyd sighed—a tribute to her mother's heart, whilst her eyes remained shrewdly observant of me." Or, as he judges his new neighbor Poirot: "There's no doubt at all about what the man's profession has been. He's a retired hairdresser. Look at that mustache of his."[13]

Dr. Sheppard's narrative voice plays up the comic qualities of the people of King's Abbot, the village of the novel, but the people themselves are "originals" in the eighteenth- or nineteenth-century manner. Most indulge in distinctive gestures, ideas, or habits of speech. Caroline minds everybody's business. Mrs. Ackroyd, the victim's sister-in-law, simpers while she ruthlessly manages. Major Blunt, the big-game hunter, almost avoids speech. Colonel Carter tells lies about the Far East. Miss Ganett cannot manage to keep up with the game of Mah Jong, which the Sheppards and their guests play to avoid the acrimony of partnerships at bridge. All coolly practice their separate foibles and calmly accept their neighbors' oddities, for as Dr. Sheppard remarks, "in King's Abbot we permit people to indulge their little eccentricities." Amusing in their own right, such characters create a strong sense of village intimacy and stability.

Poirot's stern pursuit of a dangerous misfit, a deviate hidden among the essentially harmless eccentrics, proved a winning formula, one the writer made as fully her own as Conan Doyle made the totally cerebral detective his. Many might imitate the formula, but in popular consciousness it remains Christie's.

Though *The Murder of Roger Ackroyd* was the most successful book of Agatha Christie's first decade as a writer, the next year brought the death of her mother and the collapse of her first marriage. In her next book, written out of the need for money, she had no sense of leisure in which to rework the formula. Instead, she resorted to a mechanism for stringing together several short-story plots. She recalled the situation in *An Autobiography*.

My brother-in-law, Archie's brother Campbell Christie, who had always been a great friend and was a kind and lovable person, helped me here. He suggested that the last twelve stories published in *The Sketch* should be run together, so that they would have the appearance of a book. That would be a stop-gap. He helped me with the work—I was still unable to tackle anything of the kind. In the end it was published under the title of *The Big Four*, and turned out to be quite popular. (*AA*, 341)

The situation she uses to run together the stories makes the novel as much a spy thriller as a detective novel. She pits Poirot against a Chinese of powerful intellect, an American of unlimited wealth, a Frenchwoman of scientific achievements surpassing those of Madame Curie, and an Englishman called the Destroyer.

Motivation proves the weakest element of the narrative. The Big Four, planning world domination, single out Poirot as their key adversary. How he comes to their attention remains unclear, as does his discovery of their various victims, always in the nick of time to hear about new clues.

Poirot's own movements provide the main link between the separate episodes. He scurries about England and Europe in pursuit of the Big Four and meets—in different locales—the Destroyer, master of many disguises, and the exotic Countess Rossakoff, who, like the theatrical agent Joseph Aarons, will later figure in other Christie novels and short stories. Poirot himself shaves off his mustache and pretends to be Achille, twin of Hercule.

As a novel, *The Big Four* is interesting mainly in that it demonstrates how well Agatha Christie had studied the Sherlock Holmes stories, for she freely borrows plots for the separate episodes from Conan Doyle. The novel also indicates that, if desperate to produce a book, she could anticipate the kind of pattern Ian Fleming made popular three decades later, frenzied contest between the single hero and conspiring forces of evil, though Poirot lacks James Bond's gadgetry and sexual appetites.

Her comments in *An Autobiography* suggest that although she did not care much for *The Big Four*, she had a continuing weakness for international conspiracies, as can be seen in her romantic thrillers. Fortunately, however, she kept them out of her other detective novels.

The writer herself regarded her next novel, *The Mystery of the Blue Train*, as her worst work, but she may have liked it less than *The Big Four* only because she found it harder to write. In *An Autobiography*, mulling over whether she had ever written and published a book she thought *really* bad, she confessed coming near it in *The Mystery of the Blue Train*. "Each time I read it again, I think it commonplace, full of clichés, with an uninteresting plot" (*AA*, 507).

Few would argue with the author's view that her novel was cliché-ridden, but the work is not so much commonplace as undisciplined. Instead of taking advantage of a fairly limited cast in a single setting, an approach that had sharpened her focus in *The Murder of Roger Ackroyd*, she puts Poirot in a second tale of travel, a padded version of a short story "The Plymouth Express," which was not anthologized until the 1951 collection, *The Under Dog*. The padding involves adding a string of international types, including sinister Russians, rich Americans, a Jew who allows people to think him a Greek, a French adventurer masquerading as a count, two village Englishwomen, and a few English expatriates. All highly stereotyped, these characters also assume disguises either of identity or purpose. The main plot turns on identification of the murderer of a wealthy young American woman traveling to the French Riviera by train, but Christie appends a number of subplots to her central story. One turns on the marital circumstances of the murder victim. Another involves theft of a famous ruby the victim had carried with her. Another traces the rivalry between two attractive girls for one man. Another examines the effect of sudden wealth on one of the girls. Yet another addresses Poirot's involvement with the jewel dealer. The connections among these various threads become almost as tenuous as those in her romantic thrillers.

As much as the author frankly disliked the work, *The Mystery of the Blue Train* is her first Poirot story told in the third person, and it marks the debut of one character she would use again and again, Poirot's Georges, the valet who consents to such employment because he has read that Poirot was once received at Buckingham Palace. Another character, the spinster Miss Amelia Viner of St. Mary Mead, is, like Caroline Sheppard of *The Murder of Roger Ackroyd*, a clear forerunner of Miss Marple.

The Mystery of the Blue Train falls far short of Agatha Christie's best work. Like *The Big Four*, the novel demonstrates that there are kinds of situations unsuitable for the Poirot-type character. He does not need a Hastings or even a Dr. Sheppard to recount his exploits, but a continentwide setting destroys the sense of intimacy that lets a reader participate in solving the riddle. So does too large a cast of characters. So do motives outside the range of ordinary human experience—motives such as lust for world domination. *The Big Four* and *The Mystery of the Blue Train* further suggest that Christie was more effective at providing variety when she herself invented personality types than when she relied on national types. The first prompted her comic sense as the second apparently did not.

Not all the books Agatha Christie wrote after *The Mystery of the Blue Train* were entirely satisfactory. One might, indeed, argue that a few later novels were less successful than the one she ranked as her worst. Nonetheless, by 1928 she was, by anybody's standards, a professional writer ready to begin producing detective novels at a pace and of a quality few have ever matched.

Chapter Four
Games with Form
(1930–1938)

After driving herself during a personal crisis to produce two weakly designed novel-length narratives patched up out of short story materials and two detective novels well below the standard of *The Mysterious Affair at Styles* and *The Murder of Roger Ackroyd,* between 1930 and 1938, Agatha Christie moved into the single most productive nine-year period of her career. She produced fifteen exceptionally well-constructed detective novels.

Her work during the 1930s is important not only because it includes a number of her most readable novels, but also because it illustrates two salient features of her craftsmanship: her verve in reusing, modifying, and readapting good fictive ideas and her willingness to explore new dimensions within the formulas of classic detective fiction.

Her fifteen detective novels of the period group themselves by method and content. The first five—*Murder at the Vicarage* (1930); *The Sittaford Mystery,* or *Murder at Hazelmoor* (1931); *Peril at End House* (1932); *Lord Edgware Dies,* or *Thirteen at Dinner* (1932); and *Murder on the Orient Express,* or *Murder on the Calais Coach* (1934)—all center on problems of unbreakable alibis. The next five—*Why Didn't They Ask Evans?* or *The Boomerang Clue* (1934); *Three-Act Tragedy,* or *Murder in Three Acts* (1935); *Death in the Clouds,* or *Death in the Air* (1935); *The ABC Murders* (1935); and *Murder in Mesopotamia* (1936)—have plots based on disguise. And the last—*Cards on the Table* (1936); *Dumb Witness,* or *Poirot Loses a Client* (1937); *Death on the Nile* (1937); *Appointment with Death* (1938); *Hercule Poirot's Christmas,* or *Murder for Christmas,* or *A Holiday for Murder* (1938)—are stories of individuals attempting to exert unwholesome and dangerous power over others.

That these patterns have hitherto gone unremarked is perhaps the best evidence of how well Agatha Christie could hide reused designs under varied surfaces, for within each group it is surface detail, rather

than basic plot situation, that distinguishes the novels from one another.

In *Murder at the Vicarage,* for example, the village setting and the
character of Miss Marple add a cozy flavor to a tale in which misdirection stems mainly from the murderer's seeming to have a perfect alibi. As in *The Mysterious Affair at Styles,* the murderer first seems the
obvious suspect, then appears to be exonerated, and finally is shown
to be guilty after all. As in *The Murder of Roger Ackroyd,* the villain
protects himself by creating confusion about the exact time of the
killing and by hiding among a group of suspects with strong motives.

The character who uncovers the mystery, Miss Jane Marple, is a
fluffy-haired elderly spinster first created for short stories in the late
1920s (collected in the 1932 *Thirteen Problems,* or *The Tuesday Club
Murders*). In *An Autobiography,* Agatha Christie traces the derivation
of Miss Marple from her grandmother and from "the pleasure I had
taken in portraying Dr. Sheppard's sister in *The Murder of Roger Ackroyd.* She had been my favorite character in the book—an acidulated
spinster, full of curiosity, knowing everything, hearing everything:
the complete detective service in the home" (*AA,* 420–21).

But Miss Sheppard fails to catch the significance of the details she
notices. Miss Marple is not fooled because she draws the right conclusions from her observations of such matters as flirtations, rocks offered
for a garden, or purchases in a book store. Unlike Poirot, who solves
a mystery by realizing how pieces will fit into a pattern, Miss Marple
relies on her observation of human nature from a lifetime spent in
the village of St. Mary Mead, on analogies between persons involved
in the murder and those she has known in the past, on her ability to
see through disguise and surfaces, and on her conviction that the
worst about people may well be true. In other words, she sees pieces
as parts of an already familiar pattern.

The Sittaford Mystery, or *Murder at Hazelmoor,* though also set in an
English village, has a very different texture from *Murder at the Vicarage,* but again Christie structures her tale around cracking a murderer's apparently tight alibi. Again the alibi looks good because the
murderer contrives to confuse the time of death. He leads the police
and others to believe it had to have happened while he was elsewhere
and in the company of several witnesses. Again the murderer's inat-
tention to a small physical detail undercuts his alibi.

Agatha Christie obscures the similarity of plot, especially of plot
resolution, shared by *The Sittaford Mystery* and *Murder at the Vicarage*

in part by using a very different set of characters and, indeed, a different sort of village. St. Mary Mead in *Murder at the Vicarage* has few outsiders. Snowbound Sittaford is filled with newcomers. The difference in narrative texture also arises from a change in amateur detectives. Instead of an aging Miss Marple, the writer offers Emily Trefusis, a plucky young girl of the type the writer favored in her romance thrillers. Miss Marple depends on her intimate knowledge of village life. Emily Trefusis's outsider status allows her to see clearly because she looks with fresh eyes at commonplace details.

Though providing an exceptionally simple and ingenious solution to the main puzzle of the novel, Agatha Christie complicates business with a string of subplots that may or may not have bearing on the murder itself. Why and how was the murder announced in a game of table turning at the snowbound cottage miles from the scene of the crime? Who are the lady and her daughter who have sailed from Australia under other names, and why have they chosen to spend a winter in an isolated spot near Dartmoor? Why is an attractive, energetic young woman drawn to a weakling accused of the crime, rather than to the able young reporter who admires her? Who is the newcomer to the village whose social identity puzzles all his neighbors? It seems that there is a dual purpose to these subplots: to provide cover for details of the main plot and to string out the story to its proper length. The subplots themselves, however, entail ideas repeatedly used in later Christie detective novels.

Hercule Poirot, Hastings, and Inspector Japp return for the third novel in the "perfect-alibi" group, *Peril at End House*. This time the writer employs a very different version of alibi. Instead of misleading others about the time of the crime, the culprit poses as a potential victim, a type of disguise Christie would reuse often.

One of the many Christie tales set in a resort, *Peril at End House* involves an interesting variation on the pictures of bright young things offered in the earlier romance thrillers. In those novels, the energies of the younger characters generated adventures sometimes outside a strict interpretation of the law, but usually in support of community values. In *Peril at End House,* the young appear either frivolous or wickedly self-indulgent.

Peril at End House has a less complicated set of subplots than *The Sittaford Mystery,* but like that novel it uses a number of devices and character types utilized in other Christie detective novels. The murderer seems to be a victim. The narrative is organized with a separate

chapter for each major suspect. The cast includes such typical Christiean figures as Australian colonials, a Jew who is the target of apparently unconscious English anti-Semitism, high-principled Scots, a
scholarly but abstracted clergyman, an exotic young girl with the face
of "a weary Madonna," and at least one reckless man of adventure.
Similarly, the plot turns on devices that either became staple elements
in many of Christie's narratives or else were key details in particular
stories or novels, devices such as a scrap of a letter that becomes an
important clue, a mysterious stranger who begs from his relatives in
order to satisfy a cocaine addiction, and a box of poisoned chocolates
meant to kill. Agatha Christie, in fact, had already used these devices
in *The Murder of Roger Ackroyd*. In *Peril at End House,* she also introduces new gambits that she would employ again. For example, she
makes a major issue of a shooting timed for a fireworks display, a device she would repeat in "Murder in the Mews" (1937). She uses a
death concealed so that a character can falsely secure an inheritance,
a device repeated in *A Murder Is Announced* (1950) and in *After the
Funeral,* or *Funerals Are Fatal* (1953). She makes a plot twist out of
a man's preferring a gentle plain girl to a siren, an idea reused in
"Triangle at Rhodes" (1937) and in *Evil Under the Sun* (1941).

The next novel in the perfect-alibi group, *Lord Edgware Dies,* or
Thirteen at Dinner, is set in another social milieu altogether, and the
alibi itself is of a radically different nature. It turns on an apparent
impossibility, since several witnesses swear that the primary suspect,
Lady Edgware, is in two different places at the same time. In *An Autobiography,* Agatha Christie recalled that the plot developed from her
response to a stage performance by the impersonator Ruth Draper, a
performance she had seen some time before writing the novel (*AA,*
424). In two earlier short stories, however, she had used similar plot
devices. A Tommy-Tuppence short story, "The Perfect Alibi," in
Partners in Crime, employs the same sort of confusion of identity, and
the testimony of one witness echoes a sighting from a staircase in the
Harley Quin story "The Coming of Mr. Quin," in *The Mysterious Mr.
Quin*.

The general unlovability of a majority of the characters sets *Lord
Edgware Dies* apart from most Christie novels. Lord Edgware, the victim, is a sadist perhaps involved in a homosexual relationship with
his servant. Lady Edgware, the beautiful actress Jane Wilkinson, is a
total egotist with no moral sense. The man with whom she is in love,
the Duke of Merton, is a mother-dominated prig. Edgware's daugh-

ter, Geraldine, is a repressed hater. Since these characters all have motives, each easily qualifies as a suspect, and Poirot's elimination of
false suspects becomes a process of determining who is lying about
opportunity for murder.

The characters appearing in this novel who were or would become
staple Christie personality or social types include a cowed adult
daughter, a domineering mother, an amoral beauty, a wealthy Jewish
connoisseur, a successful person deeply devoted to a dependent family
member, an improvident young aristocrat, and a pretender to culture
betrayed by a spot of ignorance. Two circumstances in the work
would also become standard bits of business: Poirot rushes to meet
someone offering vital evidence only to find him dead, and a letter
from the murderer at the end of the novel clarifies details that Poirot
has not explained. (Christie had already used this device in *The Man
in the Brown Suit* and in *The Murder of Roger Ackroyd*.) Further, in this
novel as in the later *Death on the Nile,* she has Poirot observing principal figures in a restaurant before he is involved in the mystery.

In *Murder on the Orient Express,* one of Agatha Christie's most popular works, the perfect alibi depends on several suspects sharing guilt.
The real puzzle is Poirot's search for the motive that binds together
such an apparently unlikely assortment of individuals, and the special
twist comes in Poirot's attitude toward the crime and the victim.

With the exception of *Murder on the Links, Murder on the Orient Express* represents Christie's heaviest use of real events, criminal and
otherwise. The work thus affords us a glimpse of how she adapted
reality to the purposes of detective fiction. The writer's experience
with the Simplon-Orient Express, for example, was firsthand. She had
traveled to Constantinople on this train in 1928. In December 1931,
while she was returning alone to England from her husband's dig site
in Ninevah, the train was stalled by floods. Janet Morgan, one of her
biographers, reprints a long letter Christie wrote to her husband in
which she describes fellow passengers whom she may have remembered when writing the novel. Her letter vividly sketches an American woman unfavorably comparing European travel to that in the
United States, "a thin and a *terrible* man from Chicago," a Danish
missionary lady, and a "large jocose Italian."[1] The identity of the victim in the novel, the man who had kidnapped and killed a young
child, evokes the highly publicized 1932 case of the kidnapping and
murder of Charles and Anne Morrow Lindbergh's baby son in 1932,
a crime not yet solved when Agatha Christie wrote her novel.

Christie transmutes her material from the real kidnapping into the kinds of setting and characterization that fit the requirements of classic detective fiction.

The snowbound train entirely encloses the circle of suspects, for no strangers could have come aboard. The characters of the novel are inventions, not recognizable members of the Lindbergh family. Whether or not they derive from the writer's recollection of fellow passengers on the rain-blocked train, they are national types, but unlike the caricatures of *The Mystery of the Blue Train* or *The Big Four,* they are also recognizable social types who may or may not be as harmless as they seem, who may or may not be telling the truth about themselves, who may or may not be deliberately misleading Poirot about one another. Poirot, in fact, catches each suspect in some slip in speech or in reaction to a physical object, discovering that each is capable of lying. Their lies, coupled with Poirot's brilliant guesses about the basic situation (and his knowledge of the Russian alphabet—a device from the short story "Double Sin"), trap all the witnesses into partial revelations that, added together, explain the murder. In adapting details of a real kidnapping and a real stalled train for use in her novel, Agatha Christie ingeniously stays inside the standard classic detective novel formula. She stretches the pattern, however, in her resolution, in which Poirot acts on his view that the demands of justice supersede the demands of ineffective law. Allowing no sympathy whatever for the kidnapper-murderer-victim, the writer has Poirot explain the crime only to maneuver the doctor and the wagon-lit director into agreeing to an alternate explanation that exonerates the real killers.

Though part of a group of novels turning on "perfect" alibis, *Murder on the Orient Express* submerges the basic similarity of the devices Christie uses in the group. In this novel, the motive for the crime is revenge. In other novels in the group, it had been sexual jealousy, avarice, or frustration over ego satisfaction. This variety of motives masks the recurrence of the perfect alibi device. By changing motives, or types of characters, or settings, Christie clothes her formula in different garb.

The next five detective novels—*Why Didn't They Ask Evans?* or *The Boomerang Clue* (1934); *Three-Act Tragedy,* or *Murder in Three Acts* (1935); *Death in the Clouds,* or *Death in the Air* (1935); *The ABC Murders* (1936), and *Murder in Mesopotamia* (1936)—all turn on the penetration of disguises. In an obvious sense, such penetration is a special instance of alibi breaking, but in this group, the disguises are central to the alibis.

In *Why Didn't They Ask Evans?* the criminals disguise the victim; they use disguises themselves; other suspects also assume disguises; and the young amateur detectives themselves masquerade. The *Times Literary Supplement* reviewer (27 October 1934) remarked on Christie's "playing with her characters as a kitten will play with a ball of wool, and imposing no greater strain on her readers than the pleasure of reading at a sitting a story that tickles and tantalizes but never exhausts their patience or ingenuity."[2] The reviewer clearly had patience for characters switching identities, for self-assured young amateurs bumbling into high-risk truths, and for uninhibited authorial dependence on coincidence. The hero, for example, slices his golf ball into the woods in time to hear the title question as the last words of a dying man. A photo of a "strangely haunting" face in the dead man's pocket leads the hero and his energetic, aristocratic friend, Lady Frances Derwent, to a house where Frankie becomes a houseguest by virtue of a faked accident, where the head of the household suffers from the standard upper-class vice of Christie novels, cocaine addiction, where a psychiatrist neighbor turns out to be married to a woman who matches the photograph, and where discreetly described sexual jealousy on the parts of both the hero and the heroine involve the pair in close brushes with death, as well as revelations of the whole variety of disguises worn by virtually all the characters in the narrative.

Agatha Christie followed the romance thriller–detective novel mixture of *Why Didn't They Ask Evans?* with the much tauter *Three-Act Tragedy*, or *Murder in Three Acts*, a novel featuring both Hercule Poirot and Mr. Satterthwaite, the key figure in the Harley Quin short stories. As *Murder on the Orient Express* is the most ingenious of the perfect-alibi novels, *Three-Act Tragedy* is the most complex of the disguise works.

For example, characters hide their real natures under assumed roles; the natures we suspect might be assumed are shown to be real; or, with deft double twists, those which seemed false, then real, prove false after all, and vice versa. A number of the characters are, by profession, stage people, and their professions alone cast doubt about which of their postures are real and which assumed. Sir Charles Cartwright, the actor at whose home the first murder occurs, is, as his psychiatrist friend, Dr. Bartholomew Strange, observes, "a better actor in private life than on the stage." His assumed roles in the novel include bluff seaman, M. Lupin, older man in love with young girl sentimentally giving her up, and so on. Another character, Anthony Astor, is really Muriel Wills, the homely, awkward playwright of witty, sophisticated comedy.[3] Yet another, Oliver Manders, affects rudeness to cover his own insecurities. And the young heroine, Hermione ("Egg") Lytton Gore, pretends attention to Manders to arouse Sir Charles's jealousy.

Throughout the narrative, Christie plays with false appearances in situations, as well as in characters. Young Manders stages a fake accident very like that Frankie Derwent staged in *Why Didn't They Ask Evans?* Another character, a pretended butler, fakes a disappearance. Moreover, both Poirot and the murderer manufacture false clues throughout. Poirot himself stages a false killing at a sherry party and demonstrates in the denouement that two of the real killings were red herrings to cover the motive for one crime. One killing, indeed, was committed, not to keep an individual from talking, but from announcing that he knows nothing. As a final fillip, after a conclusion in which Poirot explains the killer's actions as the product of egomania, the novel ends with this exchange between Mr. Satterthwaite and Poirot.

"My goodness," he cried, "I've only just realized it! That rascal, with his poisoned cocktail! Anyone might have drunk it. It might have been me!"

"There is an even more terrible possibility that you have not considered," said Poirot.

"Eh?"

"It might have been me," said Hercule Poirot.[4]

For *Death in the Clouds,* or *Death in the Air* (1935), Agatha Christie builds a plot of permutations of ideas from several earlier novels. She substitutes a plane for the train of *Murder on the Orient Express* in order to close her group of suspects completely. In partial echo of *Lord Edgware Dies,* she creates a chorus girl determined to prevent her aristocratic husband from divorcing her, rather than an actress bent on disposing of a husband. As in *Three-Act Tragedy,* Christie develops an ingenue who appeals to Poirot as Egg Gore had, but this one is a hairdresser rather than a member of the gentry.

Further, she varies the pattern of *Murder on the Orient Express*—in which motives are hidden—by giving too many of the passengers motives. Yet she again makes a puzzle out of *how* a murder could have been committed with so many witnesses, including Hercule Poirot, who failed to see it though they were on the scene. Also, as in *Three-Act Tragedy,* some bystanders join with Poirot to discover the murderer. While several characters prove to be wearing disguises of one sort or another, the murderer masks himself most successfully. Only Poirot, sensitive to nuances of speech, attentive to minor details, and enjoying the benefit of the blackmailing notebooks of the victim as a source for probing questions, contrives to identify him.

As evidence of the self-assurance that allowed her to be playful, Agatha Christie plants a private joke on her husband, Max Mallowan, in *Murder in the Clouds.* Inspector Japp instantly takes a pair of archaeologists for cutthroats, and the story also features a mystery writer too disorganized and muddled ever to have planned a real murder. Inadvertently, no doubt, the writer also left herself open to the kind of criticism she later humorously protested in *Cards on the Table.* There her self-caricature, Ariadne Oliver, complains about readers' fixations on accuracy with such things as blowpipes, the weapon in *Death in the Clouds.*

Though cleverly executed, *Death in the Clouds* hardly ranks as one of Christie's best efforts. She makes only limited preparation for the revelation of the murderer's identity, and the revelation requires details never offered to the reader. The novel's readability, despite its haphazard structure, demonstrates how smoothly Christie had learned to hide a weakness of motivation under artful confusion about her villain's identity, and entirely stereotypical characters under snatches of convincing dialogue.

The next novel, *The ABC Murders,* has a better puzzle than *Death in the Clouds,* and though Christie prepares an explanation for the key disguise less carefully here than she does in *Three-Act Tragedy, The ABC Murders* turns on a singularly ingenious gambit: play with a pattern of expectations built on the first three letters of the alphabet. Christie supports this gambit with elements she had earlier used in *Three-Act Tragedy.* She repeats the pattern of hiding the motivated killing among extra murders, and she again has those associated with the murder victims organize into a group to help Hercule Poirot, a group that includes the murderer himself. In *Three-Act Tragedy* Christie had made an issue of theatricality by grouping chapters into units labeled acts. In *The ABC Murders,* the alphabet idea similarly dictates narrative developments. The first victim, Alice Ascher, is killed in Andover; The second, Betty Bernard, is killed in Bexhill; and the third, Sir Carmichael Clarke, is killed in Churston. Hercule Poirot receives a letter in each case challenging him by giving the date and place of the murder, and in each case the killer leaves an ABC railroad guide under the body.

Christie achieves a different texture in this novel by mixing sections in which Hastings narrates with sections in a third-person voice that describes the suspicious behavior of one Alexander Bonaparte Custe. Most clues point toward Custe, a disturbed little man who persuades himself that he is the murderer. By not only making Custe the primary suspect, but by showing him convinced by another's machinations of his own guilt, Christie conducts her boldest game with the disguise motif. She would reuse the game in her 1952 *Mrs. McGinty's Dead,* but only in *The ABC Murders* does she sweep the reader into conviction that Poirot alone fails to share.

Although uncharacteristically casual about providing evidence to justify her surprise ending, the author provides sufficient ingenuity in the tale to make it a great favorite of critics. Julian Symon, for example, ranked *The ABC Murders* among Christie's five best novels, calling it "a masterwork of carefully concealed artifice."[5]

In *Murder in Mesopotamia,* Agatha Christie makes another new-seeming novel out of old devices. This time she tries a new kind of setting, the archaeological site of Tell Yarimiah. But she domesticates her exotic setting by peopling it with familiar character types engaged in familiar classic detective novel antics.

The old formulas in this novel include a least-likely murderer surrounded by others who prove to have motives and dubious pasts, and a pattern of sharply defined foil relationships among the characters. Again, disguise provides the major element of the plot, but with this novel the author carries off virtuoso suspension of disbelief. She defines the disguise even before the murder. The victim's first husband, a man convicted in the United States of spying for the Germans in World War I, is not dead after all, but goes on threatening his former wife. The central puzzle in the novel, complicated by a variation on the old locked-room gambit, requires fitting a character to the disguise, and the novel ends with a solution as brazen, as exuberantly imaginative, as any Christie ever invented.

She also tries out a new narrator, Nurse Leatheran, to record Hercule Poirot's investigation, and in Nurse Leatheran's voice she finds both relief from Hasting's customary adulation and an alternative to the omniscient third-person voice to which she had increasingly resorted. The matter-of-fact, unimpressed voice of Nurse Leatheran serves both to make familiar the romantic setting and situation and to generate a comic mood. Nurse Leatheran, for example, responds to the bazaars of Baghdad with imperturbable English insularity. "There's no denying they're quaint—but just a lot of rubbish and hammering away at copper pans till they make your head ache—and not what I'd like to use myself unless I was sure about the cleaning." Similarly, she is almost immune to the excitement of archaeology, re- marking, "the whole excavation looked like nothing but mud to me." Her voice reduces characters to familiar dimensions as she stresses a critical point that another character notices—"they all passed the but- ter to each other a little too politely." Setting does not keep her from noticing basic psychological facts, including the detail that the victim (apparently modeled on Katherine Woolley, the archaeologist's wife) was "the sort of woman who could easily make enemies" because of the "cool rudeness in her tone."[6]

The disguise motif as a primary explanation for criminal behavior, however clever the disguise, did not long satisfy Agatha Christie. She built her next five novels around analyses of human efforts to exert indecent power over others.

The change led to greater stress on the personalities of victims. *Cards on the Table* (1936); *Dumb Witness,* or *Poirot Loses a Client* (1937); *Death on the Nile* (1937); *Appointment with Death* (1938); and *Hercule Poirot's Christmas,* or *Murder for Christmas,* or *A Holiday for Murder* (1938) all involve victims who attempt to exercise excessive control over others. Such victims raise questions about violence that were not raised in novels that focused on disproving alibis or probing disguises, focuses that had kept the Christie detective novels safely on the plane of sanitized crime. The kinds of victims she invents for the five novels in this group, and the terms in which she defines them, reveal a shift in interest from techniques of hiding criminals among other suspects toward questions of *why* murders might be committed.

Christie never publicly explained this shift; conceivably, her atten- tion to themes of destructive love and jealousy in the two straight Mary Westmacott novels of the 1930s encouraged her to broach such issues in a string of detective novels. In any event, she produced a series of novels in which murder seems more humanly comprehensible than it had in any earlier work except for *Murder on the Orient Express.*

Though readers of this group of novels can understand why partic- ular individuals become murder victims, Christie still makes complex riddles out of who actually pulled the trigger, administered the poison, or wielded the knife. Indeed, her new favorite formula seems to have been one in which several suspects all have the same, or at least comparably strong motives.

Cards on the Table offers precisely this kind of puzzle. Interestingly, Hercule Poirot had yearned for such a case in *The ABC Murders*. " 'Supposing,' murmured Poirot, 'that four people sit down to play bridge and one, the odd man out, sits in a chair by the fire. At the end of the evening the man by the fire is found dead. One of the four, while dummy, has gone over and killed him, and intent on the play of the hand, the other three have not noticed. Ah, there would be a crime for you! *Which of the four was it?*' "[7]

The problem of an open-ended suspect list—which prompted Poirot's remark in *ABC Murders*—may have turned Agatha Christie's mind, as it turned her character's, to an idea for the opposite kind of problem—within another rigorously limited, closed circle of suspects. Or perhaps the comment was a private joke about an already planned novel. No matter, the comment sums up half the plot situation of *Cards on the Table*. A strange but compelling Mr. Shaitana gives a party for eight. Four guests are people who seem to have gotten away with murder. Four others—and this is the second half of the plot— are detectives: Hercule Poirot, Superintendent Battle, and Colonel Race from earlier Christie novels, and Ariadne Oliver, who had appeared very briefly in the Parker Pyne stories. The murderers have been playing bridge in one room, the detectives in the other, when the host, whose remarks during dinner had seemed to threaten all the murderers in turn, is found stabbed. The double puzzle entails identification of the killer and resolution of the contest among the detectives to see who can spot the killer first.

Special elements of the narrative include bridge scores as a primary clue (a device from the short story "King of Clubs"), a woman's confession that protects the young (a device the author would use in *Bertram's Hotel*), the timely prevention of a follow-up murder (a device from a number of short stories and novels), and a Faustian echo in Christie's insistent stress on Mr. Shaitana's Mephistophelian qualities (an element that figured before in the romantic thriller, *The Secret Adversary*).

Shaitana, the victim in *Cards on the Table,* bears a Near Eastern name for Satan,[8] and he fairly lures his murderer into killing him. Yet the murderer has already killed before, which leaves the emblematic point about this Satan figure a little muddled.

In fairness, Agatha Christie makes the primary business of the novel solving riddles rather than defining evil. And in *Cards on the Table* as riddle, she deftly mixes psychological suggestion with the clues of the bridge scores, scores which Poirot emphasizes enough to keep the game fair.

The issue of the victim's hunger for power and the search for the killer indicate that Christie was thinking of crime as more than an occasion for demonstrating an invented detective's power of ratiocination. But she preserves the quality of game in this novel with her apple-eating, feminist murder-mystery writer, Ariadne Oliver, whom Max Mallowan called a "lightly sketched . . . portrayal of Agatha herself."[9] Given to inventing wildly imaginative and complicated explanations of events, Mrs. Oliver complains about the pain and toil of her craft. "One actually has to *think,* you know. And thinking is always a bore. And you have to plan things."[10]

Hostilities bred by human attempts to exercise undue power over others lead, in *Death on the Nile* to a grimmer but, in some ways, a more ambitious novel than *Cards on the Table*. As usual, Christie builds her tale toward masterful twists in resolution, but she makes the puzzle element in this novel far less central than that in *Cards on the Table*. Though Hercule Poirot again works with Colonel Race, detection in *Death on the Nile* never seems a contest or a game. Even with a Near Eastern setting, and even with a woman writer and an archaeologist in the cast, the writer stays away from private jokes and self-directed irony. The writer, absolutely unlike Agatha Christie, specializes in outspoken sex, suffers a failing career, and sacrifices a daughter to her own ego. The archaeologist, Signori Richetti, proves to be a dealer in terrorist arms and has nothing in common with Max Mallowan except that he claims the same profession.

A more somber novel than *Cards on the Table, Death on the Nile* offers violent response to pressure as a predictable reaction, rather than as an exception in human conduct. Moreover, violence-prone characters easily outnumber all others in the novel. The proportion of suspects and law-abiding detectives in *Cards on the Table* was four to four. In *Death on the Nile,* Hercule Poirot and Colonel Race pit their wits against those of sixteen other characters all either trying to exercise unwarranted power or readying themselves to rebel against oppressors.

Shifting from one tersely drawn cluster of characters to another before she collects them on the cruise boat up the Nile, Agatha Christie establishes the bases for the corrosive passions among them. The primary power figure, Linnet Ridgeway, uses money and charm to get her way. Jacqueline de Bellefort uses strength of purpose. Other power figures include two dominant mothers who trade on filial duty, and a wealthy old woman who bullies dependents. Whether characters are torn by sexual jealousies or by generational power plays, the novel ends with twists that show evil taking more variant forms than readily meet the eye. Only a few characters, thanks to Hercule Poirot's nudging, escape their own destructive passions. Most destroy themselves or others in ways that illustrate Poirot's warning to one girl suffering jealousy. "Do not open your heart to evil. . . . Because if you do—evil will come. . . . It will enter in and make its home within you, and after a while it will no longer be possible to drive it out."[11]

Though *Death on the Nile* has the same title as an earlier Parker Pyne short story, similarities between the two works are matters of surface rather than substance. Both tales are set on Nile cruise boats, both involve love triangles, both have wealthy, dominant wives as victims, and both offer surprises in identification of culprits, but the short story lacks the moral and psychological underpinning of the novel. In the story, plot twists are everything; in the novel, plot supports development of an issue. The reuse of the title, in short, seems to have been simple oversight on the writer's part.

The next novel, the 1937 *Dumb Witness,* or *Poirot Loses a Client,* bears a firm connection with an earlier short story, "How Does Your Garden Grow?" The story, not anthologized until the 1939 *Regatta Mystery and Other Stories,* seems an early outline of the more elaborately developed novel, particularly in the definition of problems, the general nature of the cast of characters, and the resolution of the plots. For example, both tales begin with Poirot's receiving agitated letters from elderly ladies who place so much stress on discretion that they tell him little. In both, Poirot develops interest in the cases only when he discovers his correspondents are already dead. In both, nieces (plus a nephew in the novel) are shocked to discover their aunts have left fortunes to companions rather than relatives. Additionally, in both, Poirot must first show that the aunts' deaths have been murder rather than suicide, then discover the murderers' identities.

The fact that Agatha Christie reuses her short story materials so fully in *Dumb Witness,* and the further fact that she commits absurdities uncommon in her writing for this period of her career—absurdities such as having a nail secretly driven and varnished over just outside an open bedroom door in the dead of night without anyone's hearing or smelling anything and a suspect's wearing a large brooch on her nightdress—perhaps mean no more than that she wrote the work in haste. Nonetheless, the novel reveals her methods of spinning out a plot thread, the point, according to *An Autobiography,* from which she always began.

In *Dumb Witness,* she enlarges the cast of the short story, develops characters much more elaborately, and describes the setting in greater detail to create effects at once more humorous and more sinister in implication than those of "How Does Your Garden Grow?" She equips several characters in the novel with likely motives, and she shows the companion, both nieces, and the nephew as layered characters in whom appearances mask real natures. Their initial appearances, at least, fall into the comedy-of-manners tradition, with each character marked by distinctive mannerisms, styles of speech, or attitudes. For instance, instead of the minimally identified Russian girl who serves as the companion in the short story, Minnie of the novel pops up again and again, fussing ineffectually about household trivia, indulging in silly sentimentality, and dabbling in occultism. Though not a fully rounded character, she has enough repeatedly displayed facets to amuse readers with her predictability.

Additionally the short story offers limited scope for false leads. In the novel, the reader is led down four distinct garden paths. Finally, as one of a whole string of Christie stories and novels set in the village of Market Basing, *Dumb Witness* contains a fair number of rooms and streets described in enough detail to trigger reader imagination, if not sharply defined visual images, and these descriptions create a sense of specific place lacking in "How Does Your Garden Grow?"

In the two 1938 novels, *Appointment with Death* and *Hercule Poirot's Christmas,* or *Murder for Christmas,* or *A Holiday for Murder,* both heavy with allusions to Shakespearean tragedy, the development of the power issue threatens classic detective fiction's emphasis on emotionally cool puzzle solving. In these novels, oppressive parent figures die, and children fighting for their own identities become obvious suspects. In both, Hercule Poirot achieves surprising explanations for the deaths, explanations which somewhat muffle and defuse questions about justifiable matricide or patricide.

Agatha Christie sets *Appointment with Death* in Jerusalem and Petra, which she had visited in 1933 and which she used as the setting of the 1934 Parker Pyne short story, "The Pearl of Price." As was her custom when she reused a foreign setting, she altered her tale. In the novel, despite sharp evocative sketches of landscape such as that in the tenth chapter, Christie focuses firmly on people rather than on place. Most of the American and European characters in her larger-than-usual cast become suspects when the bullying Mrs. Boynton, traveling with her four step-children and daughter-in-law, is found dead of digitoxin poison.

In *Appointment with Death*, Agatha Christie writes a novel as much about those who tyrannize and the victims of their tyranny, as a classic, puzzle-solving work of detective fiction. Although psychiatrists fare badly in most of Christie's work, in *Appointment with Death* she creates a French psychiatrist, Dr. Gerard, who matches Poirot in analyzing characters and situations. Further, Dr. Gerard has a special sounding board in a young Englishwoman just completing her medical studies. Both professionals, and Poirot, observe in the victim, Mrs. Boynton, "a lust for power, a lust for cruelty." She has achieved such mental dominance over her step-children that they are afraid of freedom. Gerard's voice directs the reader to see her as a type of human evil. "Below the decencies and conventions of everyday life, there lies a vast reservoir of strange things. There is such a thing, for instance, as delight in cruelty for its own sake. But when you have found that, there is something deeper still. The desire, profound and pitiful, to be appreciated. If that is thwarted, if through an unpleasing personality a human being is unable to get the response it needs, it turns to other methods—it must be *felt*—it must *count*—and so to innumerable strange perversions."[12]

Although this kind of psychological theorizing serves as necessary narration, and although the denouement engineered by Poirot demonstrates the accuracy of Dr. Gerard's diagnosis, Agatha Christie observes the conventions of classic detective fiction in a restoration-of-order ending: Poirot releases the children from bondage to their mother. Moreover, Poirot as usual insists that murder is never acceptable no matter what the character of victim. "A life—taken! I say it always—I do not approve of murder." Yet Christie flirts with subverting the detective-fiction formula in her epilogue, in which the survivors meet to celebrate the youngest daughter's triumphant playing of Ophelia, the role for which Poirot has all along considered her. The epilogue first evokes the unsolvable dilemmas of Hamlet and Ophelia, then ends with lines from *Cymbeline*.

> Fear no more the heat o' the sun,
>   Nor the furious winter's rages;
>   Thou thy worldly task hast done,
>   Home art gone, and ta'en thy wages.

The grim tone of the novel notwithstanding, throughout the narrative there are flashes of Agatha Christie's increasingly assured wicked comic sense, especially in her sketches of secondary figures. The twittery Miss Price traps herself into pretending to be stalwart; the brusque Colonel Carbury gets caught between wanting Poirot to solve the crime and preferring to see justification for his distrust of the detective's "un-British" attitudes; and the arrogant Lady Westholme sails into a room "with the assurance of a transatlantic liner coming into dock" and lectures one and all on her watchword, "efficiency." The special vividness of Lady Westholme, indeed, prompts commentators to look for a real life model. Charles Osborne proposes Lady Astor,[13] and Janet Morgan suggests "the excessively fierce-looking Miss Wilbraham," whom Agatha had encountered leading a party of Anglo-Catholics to Iraq in the spring of 1930.[14]

In using a domestic English setting and in developing a tyrannical father figure rather than a mother figure for *Hercule Poirot's Christmas,* Agatha Christie wrote a novel different from *Appointment with Death* in feel and method of solution, but not in theme. She also omits open psychoanalysis of characters and develops a far stronger riddle element in *Hercule Poirot's Christmas* than she had in *Appointment with Death*.

As the dedication to her brother-in-law, James Watts, indicates, she set out to give the murder element of the novel prominence. "You complained that my murders were getting too refined—anaemic, in fact. You yearned for a 'good violent murder with lots of blood.' A murder where there was no doubt about its being murder!"[15]

In no way could the death of Simeon Lee, master of Gorston Hall, have been natural, though Dennis Sanders and Len Lovallo remark, "A 'good violent murder' is for Agatha best pictured in the disarray of furniture, irreparably stained Oriental rugs, and lovely Ming porcelains shattered into a million shards."[16] To details about the wreckage of a room she adds a quotation from *Macbeth*. "Who would have thought the old man to have had so much blood in him." Then she sets up the traditional sealed-room gambit and adds complications with a batch of missing uncut diamonds.

Simeon Lee's children are less obviously his victims than Mrs. Boynton's children had been hers, but even so they all have good reasons for killing him. Alfred, the eldest, has spent a lifetime trying to please him and being scorned for his pains. Alfred's wife, Lydia, has never pretended to like her father-in-law. Son Harry, appearing after a twenty-year absence, is a ne'er-do-well who has always bent the law. Son George, pompous member of Parliament with a young expensive wife, could not manage with the cut in allowance his father threatens. Son David, an artist driven by memories of his victim mother, has thought of avenging her for twenty years, and David's sensible wife, Hilda, may be capable of doing anything for the husband she mothers. Then there are others whose identities may be false: a half-Spanish granddaughter ready to slit the throats of enemies, a South African son of Simeon's old partner, and other illegitimate offspring at whose existence Simeon likes to hint.

The allusions to *Macbeth* prepare the reader for one of Agatha Christie's starker detective puzzles, one with few flashes of humor and the most limited kind of links with her other fiction. In fact, the only other Hercule Poirot story alluded to directly is *The ABC Murders,* a rather interesting omission after the cross-references to *The ABC Murders, Cards on the Table,* and *Murder on the Orient Express* in *Appointment with Death.*

Perhaps in *Murder for Christmas,* Christie took one kind of experiment with her form about as far she wanted. For in her next group of novels, she moved again in a new direction.

Chapter Five
The War Years
(1939–1947)

In 1939, beginning with *Murder Is Easy* (or *Easy to Kill*) and *Ten Little Niggers* (or *And Then There Were None,* or *Ten Little Indians,* or, in Nairobi, *Ten Little Redskins*),[1] Agatha Christie backed away from narratives in which power-grasping victims posed sufficient danger to deserve being killed, and in which the competence or rectitude of the law was questioned. Having ducked the issue of justifiable homicide in *Appointment with Death* only by using a nonrepeatable surprise ending, and having set up a twist in *Hercule Poirot's Christmas* she could not use again without inviting questions about the difference between criminal and law enforcer, Christie returned to narratives in which mystification, the whodunit question in its most complicated form, became the key issue.

She may have refocused on pure puzzle novels because she sensed that her tales about obsession and power grabbing threatened the basic premises of her special form. Poirot's defensive explanations in both *Appointment with Death* and *Hercule Poirot's Christmas* suggest authorial anxiety lest his role as agent of right and justice be compromised.

Or public events in 1938 and 1939, the coming of World War II, may have prodded her to return to firm classic detective novel formulas as a kind of response-by-denial to the real violence threatening Britain and much of the world. In writing detective novels in which decent, clearheaded individuals could recognize and expel disruptive elements, she affirmed, in a sense, the vitality of civilized social patterns. The reasoning individual, the thinking detective, could apprehend and isolate the source of disruption, the maverick agent of violence. By casting him out, other ordinary members of society could live securely and happily. More basically, the values embodied in British law would be shown to grant dignity and significance to those capable of accepting community standards. Justice and right could and would prevail.

Agatha Christie's detective novels had always been escape literature in the sense that they were morality tales in which evil was defeated. They had, further, provided the kind of escape implicit in neatly patterned, Aristotelian beginnings, middles, and endings. But as World War II began, Christie made her detective fiction escapist in another sense. She systematically avoided allusion to current events and set a string of particularly complex puzzles in a clearly prewar era. Her hold over British readers surviving the actual disruption and horrors of the blitz indicates that her celebrations of the triumph of ratiocination spoke to her countrymen, both as welcome distractions and as subtle testaments of faith that simpler, saner times would come again.

Murder Is Easy initially calls into question the basic order of British life, for the writer invents a village seething with sinister forces. Yet the novel affirms order and traditional values in that a single wicked person turns out to be responsible for apparently rampant evil. Until the denouement, almost every character, except for the narrator and the first victim, figures as a plausible suspect at one time or another. The murderer could be the childishly egocentric, self-made newspaper mogul, the homosexual dabbler in antiques and witchcraft, the arrogant doctor, the bereaved mother trying to profit from talking about her dead son, the brutal innkeeper, or the Irish girl who looks like a witch and seems to be marrying for money. But despite character flaws in the villagers, only one is a killer, and that killer, in fact, has helped generate damaging interpretations of others.

Christie's misdirection in *Murder Is Easy* depends heavily on the plausibility of all her suspects, but she also uses a variety of other basic detective-fiction tricks: setting up the reader to assign the murderer's real motive to the wrong person, having characters in the story look in the wrong directions, letting the investigator—and the reader—jump to the wrong conclusions about the meaning of a single key word.

In *Ten Little Niggers,* the writer played one of the trickiest games she ever invented, adding a new level of artifice to her already highly stylized form by structuring her tale around a nursery rhyme in which all characters, one by one, are eliminated. The rhyme itself committed her to inventing means of murder that could, with some plausibility, correspond to such lines as "One chopped himself in halves and then there were six," or "A bumblebee stung one and then there were five," or "A big bear hugged one and then there were two." The second, and perhaps greatest, part of the challenge required her hiding the killer's identity in a rapidly closing circle by her use of such misleading devices as characters misdirecting each other—and the reader—as each guesses at the killer's identity; the killer's offering false clues; his confusing times; and his faking his own death. A reader who pays very close attention to nuances of phrasing may spot him, but the whole plot is a tour de force of hiding a tree in a forest. Agatha Christie herself remarked: "I had written the book . . . because it was so difficult to do that the idea had fascinated me. Ten people had to die without it becoming ridiculous or the murderer being obvious. I wrote the book after a tremendous amount of planning, and I was pleased with what I had made of it. . . . I knew better than any critic how difficult it had been" (*AA*, 457).

Christie would eventually come to doubt whether she was right in making one of her 1940 novels, *Sad Cypress*, a detective novel. Late in her career, in a 1966 interview with Francis Wyndham, she confessed: "*Sad Cypress* could have been good, but it was quite ruined by having Poirot in it. I always thought *something* was wrong with it, but didn't discover what till I read it again some time after."[2]

As written, however, *Sad Cypress* is a whodunit with standard kinds of apparatus and gimmicks. It begins with the central figure in the dock, accused of murdering the aunt who left her a fortune. Evidence against her seems overwhelming, but Poirot saves her from the gallows by identifying the real criminal in a brilliant reexamination of clues. Poirot's exposition of events in the denouement dominates the narrative, and his analysis makes the novel primarily a tale of ratiocination, despite the fact that he solves the mystery by discovering that key human relationships have not been what they seemed.

Without Poirot, the story thread unquestionably would be the stuff of which the author made Mary Westmacott novels—a situation in which a character who loves without suspicion or reserve discovers the object of such love to be incapable of returning it, in which greed sours love, in which the past still shapes events. Poirot's presence keeps the novel in the realm of detective fiction because he functions *as* a detective, finding clues by carefully weighing what characters say, where they have been at critical times, and what they are trying to hide.

Agatha Christie might have found a way to resolve *Sad Cypress* without Poirot's exposition, but his little grey cells are essential in the other 1940 novel, *One, Two, Buckle My Shoe* (or *The Patriotic Mur-*

ders, or *An Overdose of Death*). In *One, Two, Buckle My Shoe,* Christie repeats the trick of *Ten Little Niggers,* again using a nursery rhyme gambit. Correspondences between the rhyme and the detective novel in the second exercise, however, are looser, less surprisingly apropos than they had been before. In *One, Two, Buckle My Shoe,* the writer fools the reader, as she had in *Ten Little Niggers,* by supplying him with many likely suspects. Her cast includes a new embodiment of Caroline Sheppard from *The Murder of Roger Ackroyd;* a hard-drinking, quick-witted, charming Irishman; a mysterious rich Greek; a pushy American woman; her pretty aggressive daughter; a young American radical; an Anglo-Indian woman of limited sense but good intentions; a Cockney lad; a lower-class ne'er-do-well; his earnest, hardworking girl friend; an important banker; and a retired intelligence agent. Christie collects most of this crowd in the office of a dentist who is murdered almost under Poirot's nose. She also develops a killer who confuses the times of his multiple murders, characters wearing disguises, uncertainty about who was intended as victim, and a murderer playing hound instead of hare.

So neatly structured a whodunit that John Cawelti used it to illustrate the proper balance of the form, balance between mystification and detection, between a clear course of events and concealed clues,[3] *One, Two, Buckle My Shoe* also develops a complex theme. In solving the riddle, Poirot confronts divided loyalties—to one's social class versus one's country, to judicial principle versus national need. These issues obviously touch upon concerns heightened by Britain's wartime situation, but the writer avoids any detail that would place her tale in any particular time period. Poirot, though troubled by concern for the nation, finds guidance for his own choices, not in the fact of wartime strains, but in the Scriptures, in a reading from the psalms during an Anglican service. (Poirot, *bon catholique,* as he often describes himself, seems curiously familiar with the service.)

Evil under the Sun, another pure classic detective story like *Ten Little Niggers,* also has an enclosed island setting. The plot blends elements of two short stories of the 1930s: "The Bloodstained Pavement," in which a couple kill a string of women the man marries for insurance; and "Triangle at Rhodes," in which only Poirot rightly identifies the points of an eternal triangle. However, Christie openly links the novel not to these short stories but to the novel, *Death on the Nile.* A report from Cornelia Robson of that novel establishes Poirot's reputation, and Poirot's assessment of the situation somewhat ungrammatically links the plots. "And Hercule Poirot, with a sigh, said as he had said once before in Egypt, that if a person is determined to commit murder it is not easy to prevent them."[4]

Evil under the Sun, much longer than the short stories, presents a better puzzle than either. It includes more likely suspects and more artful misdirection, and Christie indulges in broader social comedy, as background figures holidaying on the Devon coast exhibit themselves. Further, she makes an issue of teasing her reader. In every Poirot novel, the little detective speaks at length about his methods, and the author uses his boasts to invite the reader to match wits with him. Never, however, did she use the device more heavily than in *Evil Under the Sun,* in which Poirot talks constantly of assembling the pieces of the mosaic or puzzle. The reiteration of odd details challenges the reader to discover the explanation the detective keeps claiming to have seen.

In 1940 Agatha Christie began two novels planned for posthumous publication. *Curtain,* published in 1975, shortly before her death, would bear the subtitle, *Poirot's Last Case; Sleeping Murder,* a last case for Miss Marple, was actually published in 1976. Both were written for family members. As she explained in *An Autobiography*:

> Besides what I have already mentioned, I had written an extra two books during the first years of the war. This was in anticipation of my being killed in the raids, which seemed to be in the highest degree likely as I was working in London. One was for Rosalind, which I wrote first—a book with Hercule Poirot in it—and the other was for Max—with Miss Marple in it. Those two books, when written, were put in the vaults of a bank, and were made over formally by deed of gift to Rosalind and Max. They were, I gather, heavily insured against destruction.
>
> "It will cheer you up," I explained to them both, "when you come back from the funeral, or the memorial service, to think that you have got a couple of books, one belonging to each of you!" (*AA,* 497)

The writer's key purpose in *Curtain,* like Arthur Conan Doyle's on an earlier occasion, appears to have been the killing off of a series detective lest others take him over. In her early fifties when she wrote the novel, Christie presumably was deliberately vague about dating, but she made an issue of the symmetry between *Curtain* and the first Poirot work, *The Mysterious Affair at Styles.* Again, events occur at Styles Court—though the house has been converted into a guest house; again Hastings narrates the tale—though he is an older if not wiser widower; and again the pair engage in their old forms of banter—though their responses to the old jokes tend to turn into sad recollections.

The tale itself presents a subtler ratiocinative puzzle, with far fewer significant physical clues than Christie had used in her first novel. Its key issues are whether, and how, Poirot can trap an Iago-like villain, one who moves others to murder without participating directly himself. Thus, *Curtain* allows much greater attention to Poirot's own mental processes than did *Styles*. Also, the writer's prose style had become cleaner, plainer, and less adverbial. She had also developed a surer touch at indicating character with gesture and fragments of speech.

Yet in comparison with Christie novels written after the 1940s, *Curtain* lacks social detail and humorous character sketches. The writer creates an uncharacteristically somber tone, in part because she draws a dying Poirot, in part because all the other characters have, in one way or another, been defeated or disillusioned by life.

The mood of *Sleeping Murder* is lighter than that of *Curtain,* even though Christie builds the work around a line from that grim Jacobean tragedy, Webster's *Duchess of Malfi.* Miss Marple does not die, and despite a high level of hocus-pocus with submerged memories and incestuous feelings, the novel ends with a perfectly rational explanation of events. The plot, in fact, turns on a demonstration that the heroine has neither dreamed nor made up disturbing impressions; instead, she has remembered in spite of herself.

The narrative exhibits an especially neat version of simultaneous forward movement (the heroine's current anxiety, which eventually leads to an attempt on her own life) and backward movement (development of an explanation for an eighteen-year-old murder). In fact, in unraveling the old crime, the novel anticipates the 1943 *Five Little Pigs,* or *Murder in Retrospect.* The second novel-length Miss Marple tale in terms of date of composition, *Sleeping Murder* also offers a marvelously reductive comedy when Miss Marple finally defeats the murderer. She blinds him with the syringe she had been using to get rid of greenfly on roses.

In the 1942 Miss Marple novel, *The Body in the Library,* Agatha Christie ignores World War II as totally as she had in *Sleeping Murder.* She creates a prewar village setting that allows her to make a key issue out of whether Miss Marple's friend, Colonel Bantry, can be implicated in the murder of a young woman found dead in his library. Christie weaves her story around issues of social identity, such as whether the Bantrys will suffer unjust ostracism, whether a man crippled in an accident might be defrauded by a common young girl, whether a well-born young man with a loose life-style is or is not honoring the code to which he was born, and whether certain fortune hunters will be successful.

With all its issues, *The Body in the Library* is a romp through pure detective fiction (with a title attributed to Ariadne Oliver in *Cards on the Table*). In a finely paced opening chapter, a maid tries to convince the Bantrys that she has seen a body in their library, while Colonel Bantry splutters that bodies are always found in libraries in books, but never in real life. From the self-directed fun of this chapter, Christie lays out her special comedy-of-manners never-never land of secure English village life, in which greed, lust, and other inevitable human vices surface, but then yield to common sense and strong community values. Miss Marple herself remorselessly affirms that she feels quite pleased to think of the murderer's being hanged.

The ending of *The Body in the Library* surprises less than those of most Christie classics, and for this reason the reader used to her tricks runs the greatest risk of being fooled. In the novel, she has the likeliest suspect turn out to be the killer, and she puts the main clues, with one notable exception, so much out in the open that Christiephiles may think them red herrings.

Agatha Christie listed the 1942 *Moving Finger* among the three detective novels that pleased her most (*AA,* 507). Though Miss Marple, who enters the story only at the end, supplies a solution for the puzzle, the narrating central figure is a young man recovering from a flying accident. Accompanied by his chic sister, he seeks rest in Lymstock, a village stirring with violent feeling under its placid surface, a village plagued by a poison-pen letter writer.

Christie does several things well in the novel. She misdirects fairly but with maddening ease. Her characters remain humanly interesting even when exhibiting the kinds of flaws that make them possible suspects. She shows special finesse in inviting the reader to *like* them as people once he has discarded them as potential murderers. She also treats her romantic interest with more humor than sentimentality, allowing the hero to play Pygmalion with his awkward young lady.

By 1938 Agatha Christie had admitted to her publisher that she found Hercule Poirot "rather insufferable,"[5] but she continued to use him for novels that set up special challenges for him as a detective and for her as a writer. In *Five Little Pigs,* or *Murder in Retrospect* (1943), Poirot solves the sixteen-year-old murder of artist Amyas

Crale, whose wife Caroline, now dead, had been convicted of killing him. At the instigation of the Crales' daughter, Poirot collects and assesses the variant accounts of the five people who remember the affair. And because he notices nuances and details others had overlooked, he discovers the truth.

Most Christie commentators praise *Five Little Pigs* for its complex characterization, and some find correspondences between Agatha and Archie Christie before their divorce and the Crales in the novel.[6] But the real skill of the narrative lies in the adroit overlapping of five oral and five written accounts of interested parties. The writer beats the odds by keeping her tale alive despite the necessary repetitions, and she hides her clues in turns of phrase.

As connoisseurs value *Five Little Pigs* for its characterization, they value *Towards Zero,* or *Come and Be Hanged* (1944), for its structural complexities. Never before had Agatha Christie played so freely with episodic foreshadowing. Early in the novel, she uses two seemingly unconnected, unrelated episodes to warn the reader how to spot the murderer. First, Superintendent Battle discovers that his daughter has been wrongly accused of theft and that her schoolmistress, practicing shallow psychology, has hounded her into false confession. Sylvia Battle's experience anticipates the false assumptions that others in the novel, and presumably the reader, hold about the killer in the main story. Then a foiled suicide anticipates the end of the novel and deepens the premise that destiny links individuals in ways they cannot foretell.

Christie's device of marking segments by dates during an eight-month period underscores the idea that events relentlessly converge as Lady Tressilian finds herself hostess to her husband's nephew, the nephew's current wife, his former wife, and assorted others.

At midpoint in the novel, the elderly attorney tells a story about a child with an unnamed physical peculiarity who deliberately killed another child and whose nature may not have changed. The attorney is found dead, presumably from heart failure, and shortly afterward Lady Tressilian is killed, presumably with a golf club. These murders actually constitute Mrs. Christie's new twist on her usual puzzle pattern. In most of her novels, midpoint murders occur because the killer tries to cover up his principal murder. In *Towards Zero* he only builds toward it.

Agatha Christie offers one other fair pointer for discovering the criminal, when a character muses that murder mysteries usually begin with murder yet adds: "But murder is the *end*. The story begins long before that—years before, sometimes—with all the causes and events that bring certain people to a certain place at a certain time on a certain day—in other words, towards zero."[7]

Many clues to the killer's identity, however, have been offered prior to the murders of either of the first two victims, that is, before the reader has learned what to look for. Other clues, such as the reference to a physical peculiarity, could apply to more than one suspect. Finally, the killer creates one of the most effective smokescreens in the Christie canon, a smokescreen that includes setting up suspicion of another, appearing to have an alibi, and seeming to have less motive than any other suspect.

Agatha Christie's next novel, the 1945 *Death Comes at the End,* was a remarkable once-only experiment that reflected both her interest in ancient history and her conviction that human nature is constant. In *An Autobiography,* she reported that she was between writing projects when Professor Stephen Glanville, Egyptologist and friend of the Mallowan family, talked her into writing a detective story about ancient Egypt. She agreed on the grounds that "people are the same in whatever century they live, or where." Glanville supplied books and gave her a couple of days to pick a period. Choosing between an incident from the Fourth Dynasty, one from the later Rameses, and one suggested in letters published in the 1920s from a Ka priest in the Eleventh Dynasty, she chose the third. Since Glanville had started her on the book, for weeks and months she badgered him with questions about details of daily Egyptian life, and in return for his assistance, she changed her original denouement to fit his ideas. Without indicating what her own ending had been, she wrote: "In this case, against my better judgment, I *did* give in. It was a moot point, but I still think now, when I reread the book, that I would like to rewrite the end of it—which shows that you should stick to your guns in the first place, or you will be dissatisfied with yourself' (*AA,* 482–84).

Death Comes at the End focuses on a family dominated by an overbearing father and torn by sibling rivalries. This basic situation, despite the exotic setting, echoes the 1938 *Hercule Poirot's Christmas,* except that this later novel has no detective figure. Members of the family themselves sort out who among them is a killer, but as in *Ten Little Indians,* the circle of suspects grows ever smaller, for the likeliest early suspects themselves become victims.

Agatha Christie makes her ancient Egyptian family seem as alive as the denizens of English villages like St. Mary Mead. In fact, they are the same sorts of people with different kinds of names, dress, and patterns of daily life. As a puzzle novel, however, *Death Comes at the End* lacks clues pointing to the resolution, perhaps because the writer had not planned for the ending she used. A Christie addict may amuse himself with guessing, from internal evidence, what her original plan for a surprise might have been.

In her next detective novel, *Sparkling Cyanide,* or *Remembered Death* (1945), Agatha Christie makes another complex puzzle out of a re- used, but altered, basic plot, that of the short story "Yellow Iris." The same core group of renamed characters meet in a renamed restau- rant on the anniversary of an ostensible suicide, and another person dies exactly as the first victim had. Colonel Race replaces Hercule Poirot as the investigator who discovers who killed both.

Neither these changes nor the writer's picking a different character for the guilty party changes the basic pattern of both narratives. Her real modification involves narrative method. The short story offers a taut line of development: the suspects gather, the murder occurs, and Hercule Poirot knows who is guilty because he has paid more atten- tion than anyone else to everybody's movements. The story line in the novel seems much more complex because Christie lays out almost equally plausible motives for the earlier killing in the recollections of six separate characters. When the second victim dies, the reader must choose among these six, plus others to whose minds he has had less access. Additionally, the writer spins out the plot thread with six dif- ferent love relationships, using the tensions these generate to cover her clues.

Continuing her pattern of hiding a murderer among a closed circle of suspects, in *The Hollow,* or *Murder after Hours* (1946), Christie in- vents a tale in which discovery of the culprit depends less on adding up bits of physical evidence than on recognizing psychological possi- bilities. Despite Poirot's boasts about his ability to recognize murder- ers by studying the psychology of both the victim and the killer, *The Hollow* is one of the novels in which Christie regretted Poirot's pres- ence. As she explained: "*The Hollow* was a book I always thought I had ruined by the introduction of Poirot. I had got used to having Poirot in my books, and so naturally he had come into this one, but he was all wrong there" (*AA,* 458).

Like the other detective novels in which she regretted using Poirot, *The Hollow* sets out a pattern of contrasting love relationships: one partner loves more intensely than another; one relationship is passion- ate; another is comfortable. Like the early Harley Quin stories, the

Twayne's English Authors Series

Agatha Christie

Mary S. Wagoner

novel also deals with opposition between the pulls of ordinary life and those of artistic intensity.

Because these contrasts and oppositions serve as clues to the narrative's puzzle, they do not seem alien to the detective-novel form. But the characters of *The Hollow* indulge in the sort of stilted posturing the writer could get away with only when she took a comic view.

Despite the stylized characters, the story is located in a particularized and real setting, as her dedication reveals: "For Larry and Danae, with apologies for using their swimming pool as the scene of a murder." According to Gwen Robyns's *Mystery of Agatha Christie,* Larry—Francis L. Sullivan, the actor who played Poirot in *Black Coffee* and again in *Peril at End House*—actually caught the writer planning the discovery of the body. Half a dozen paths led through the chestnut wood to the Sullivan's pool. "One fine Sunday morning," Mr. Sullivan reported, "I discovered Agatha wandering up and down these paths with an expression of intense concentration."[8]

After *The Hollow,* her fourteenth detective novel in a decade, Christie published an anthology of short stories and a Westmacott novel, but no new detective novels. With *Taken at the Flood,* or *There Is a Tide,* in 1948, as though released from the restraints that had kept references to current events out of her work during the war, she began writing specifically topical novels, mixing details of postwar pressures on people's lives with her old tricks of characterization and plot development.

Chapter Six
Postwar Work
(1948–1958)

After World War II, Agatha Christie became more experimental, adapting her form to a changing social scene. Though her detective novels became less predictably able, she produced several singularly fine tales.

Her first work of this period, *Taken at the Flood,* is gripping narrative that combines many of her earlier interests with a postwar setting. The novel draws the extended Cloade family, a group comparable to the Lee tribe of *Hercule Poirot's Christmas*: siblings of different temperaments, married to different kinds of mates, pursue diverse life-styles. Like the Lees, the Cloades are accustomed to the financial support of the head of their family. But parallels between the Lees and the Cloades break down, marking the contemporary element of *Taken at the Flood.* The head of the Cloade family has been killed in the blitz, shortly after marrying a young wife. She inherits the money his dependents always assumed he would leave them. Exhausted by wartime strains, the older Cloades lack the energy to cope with the loss of their economic and social securities. The younger Cloades have an additional problem. Not only has their world changed, but they have changed themselves. The heroine, after her own service abroad, returns to a fiancé who was excused from military duty. She finds fitting into her old role extremely difficult, but so does her young man, who resents not having gone off to war. The analysis of another young person by Superintendent Spence, a new figure in the Christie police gallery, elucidates to some extent, the circumstances of all the young. "In wartime, a man like that is a hero. But in peace—well, in peace such men usually end up in prison. They like excitement and they can't run straight, and they don't give a damn for society—and finally they've no regard for human life."[1]

As the issue of social dislocation makes suspects of many characters, so it also accounts for the key riddle of the novel, the identity of the victim. He may have been the first husband of Cloade's widow, a husband from whom she was never divorced. This man had registered at the village inn as Enoch Arden. Around his identity, and the involvement of each of the Cloades in his death, the writer spins an exceptionally complex puzzle, with kaleidoscopic arrangement and rearrangement of clues. Her tricks include shifting suspicion from most-likely to least-likely possibilities and back again; demonstrating that no individual's story is entirely true; providing an exceptionally large number of red herrings; a similarly large number of rather forthright verbal clues buried in conversations that seem irrelevant to murder; and elaborately shuffling evidence about which of the three deaths is suicide, which accident, and which murder.

In the 1949 *Crooked House*, Agatha Christie again demonstrates that her old tricks still work even when her reference points are topical. She returns to a nursery rhyme for a title, if not for a structure. She also again identifies two major characters, a man and a woman, as returned veterans, but she makes the main issue of her narrative something other than postwar adjustment. Substituting for Poirot a young man whose father is assistant commissioner of police at Scotland Yard, she invents another diverse, extended family group, as she had in *Taken at the Flood*.

The ending of *Crooked House*, however, differs significantly from that of *Taken at the Flood*. Christie has a new kind of murderer who kills from a motive the writer had never before used. Further, despite a loose parallel with the short story "The Chocolate Box," she introduces a new element in the fate of the murderer, though the underlying idea lurks in many of her other detective novels: some individuals are born with the kinds of imbalances in personality that make them killers. She defines murderers as psychological mutants, bad seed. Murderers lack the brake that operates on most people. "A child," the Scotland Yard man remarks, "translates desire into action without compunction. A child is angry with its kitten, says 'I'll kill you,' and hits it on the head with a hammer—then breaks its heart because the kitten didn't come alive again! . . . But some people, I suspect, remain morally immature. They continue to be aware that murder is wrong, but they do not feel it."[2]

Such an assumption has obvious advantages for classic detective fiction. It precludes sociological questions that might diffuse guilt, and it raises few awkward issues about the propriety of punishing criminals by excluding them, if not by hanging them. In fact, the

idea that a criminal is born, and the companion idea that the importance of criminal investigation arises from its protecting the innocent
more than from its discovering the guilty, perhaps account for the
writer's identifying *Crooked House* and *Ordeal by Innocence* (1958) as the
two detective books that satisfied her best (*AA,* 506). She chose
the two novels in which she had pursued these theories most openly
and most systematically. She may have been more committed to defending these hypotheses than her critics have generally recognized.

In her next two detective novels, *A Murder Is Announced* (1950) and
Mrs. McGinty's Dead (1953), Agatha Christie turned from family
groups to community groups and began chronicling changes in daily
English life. In *A Murder Is Announced,* for example, she draws the
old upper middle class at bay in the village of Chipping Cleghorn.
They have adapted themselves to barter and black market, to housing
shortages, to offspring who read the *Daily Worker* or gardeners who
are young women, but they struggle with the problem of neighbors
they no longer know. As Miss Marple remarks: "Every village and
small country place is full of people who've just come and settled
there without any ties to bring them. The big houses have been sold,
and the cottages have been converted and changed."[3]

In *A Murder Is Announced,* Christie uses the new transience of English village life to whip up a mystery that depends heavily on false
identities, false names, and false assumptions about names. And she
ties questions about whether people are what they seem, or claim to
be, to companion questions about whether they see what they think
they see.

In the arresting beginning of the novel, villagers discover an item
in the personals column of the local newspaper that reads: "A murder
is announced and will take place on Friday, October 29, at Little Pad-
docks, at 6:30 p.m. Friends please accept this, the only intimation."
Assuming a murder game, they gather to make nicely tuned small
talk. On the hour, the lights go out, a man with a flashlight opens
the door, calls "Stick 'em up," three shots ring out, and the man falls
dead to the floor.

Discovering who shot him and why becomes the business of Miss
Marple, luckily visiting in the neighborhood. Critics have complained about the circumstances of her discovery, for it involves uncommonly heavy coincidence for a Christie novel. It also involves
gimmicks Christie had used in early short stories, namely substitute
identities, reminiscent of those in "The Companions," and a trick

mimicking voice to trap a killer from "A Death on the Nile." On key points, however, readers can only blame themselves for missing the plain verbal clues. And many may judge that the wryly amusing sketches of ordinary English folk going about their ordinary business outweigh a little hocus-pocus in the denouement.

The 1953 *Mrs. McGinty's Dead*, or *Blood Will Tell*, shows Agatha Christie giving old formulas a fresh look by widening her social range. Here Hercule Poirot, first seen dining in a restaurant, as he had been in *Taken at the Flood*, yields to the request of Superintendent Spence from that novel that he investigate the murder of a domestic, a murder for which her unprepossessing boarder has already been tried and convicted. The writer had launched *Five Little Pigs* and *Sad Cypress* with similar retrospective investigations. For *Mrs. McGinty's Dead*, she also revives Ariadne Oliver for her first appearance in a Christie novel in sixteen years. Together, Poirot and Mrs. Oliver unravel the affairs of the village of Broadhinny, but these affairs, unlike those of the Christie novels of the 1920s and 1930s, involve working-class folk and "new" people, as well as old gentry. Further, as in *A Murder Is Announced*, the puzzle is complicated by the fact that villagers really do not know one another. No one can even be certain that anybody is using his own real name.

Agatha Christie finds an ingenious device for emphasizing this point. Poirot's investigation turns on an intriguing clue that the convicted man might not have been the murderer. A sensational newspaper clipping, found among the dead woman's possessions, describes several women involved in murder cases in the past and asks "where are they now?" On inspection, most females in the village might be one of the missing women. Nearly killed himself after displaying pictures from the clipping, Poirot surmises that the woman wearing a disguise must be the killer, but identification depends on information he gathers from Australia. When the information comes, the real surprise depends on the reader's having shared a false assumption with the characters in the novel. This assumption, in fact, echoes that which hid the answer in *A Murder Is Announced*.

The extent to which Christie combines mutations and permutations of old tricks with new-seeming characters in *Mrs. McGinty's Dead* demonstrates how easily she can fool us again and again if she changes the surface of her formulas. Actually, she makes a self-mocking game of reuse. Poirot fairly parodies himself, both in his agonized complaints about chaotic life in a guest house incompetently run by

Major John Summerhayes and his wife, the last of the village gentry, and in his garbled English idioms and metaphors. Christie also plays with irony at her own expense in the character of Ariadne Oliver. A playwright adapting one of Mrs. Oliver's novels for the stage drives her to distraction as, according to *An Autobiography,* adaptors usually affected Agatha Christie. Then, Mrs. Oliver reviews her own novels in a tone very like that her creator was wont to use. Looking at a Penguin display of her works, Mrs. Oliver muses: *"The Affair of the Second Goldfish* . . . that's quite a good one. *The Cat It Was Who Died*—that's where I made a blowpipe a foot long and it's really six feet. . . . Oh! *Death of a Debutante*—that's frightful tripe . . . at least eight people die before Sven Hjerson gets his brainwave."[4] Mrs. Oliver's impatience with *her* detective Sven plainly corresponds to Christie's professed boredom with Poirot. "How do I know why I ever thought of the revolting man? I must have been mad! Why a Finn when I know nothing about Finland? Why a vegetarian? Why all the idiotic mannerisms he's got? . . . Fond of him? If I met that bony, gangling, vegetable-eating Finn in real life, I'd do a better murder than any I've invented."[5]

With less self-directed play, Agatha Christie builds a tale around the issue of effective illusions in her second 1952 detective novel, *They Do It with Mirrors,* or *Murder with Mirrors.* Featuring Miss Marple, the novel is set in another large house that shelters an extended and diverse family group.

As a puzzle, *They Do It with Mirrors* ranks well below the Christie best in ways that help define that best. The problem arises not from the nature of the puzzle itself, but from the reader's access to clues for solving it. That is, in this novel, until Miss Marple sees through and explains the murderer's carefully staged appearances (based on her detection of likenesses between suspects and villagers whose flaws in character she has long studied), the reader has only false clues with which to work. Other characters, including police investigators, do not suspect the real culprit. Several suspects have obvious motives and twists in personality. In fact, few Christie novels have as many identifiable criminals, for the family in question runs a permissive reform school for delinquent boys. The real murderer stays in the background, and the writer offers no early hints, not even that the real murderer was not where he was reported to be when the murder was committed. Nor does she offer plain clues about the identity of his accomplice. Moreover, the characters, except perhaps Miss Marple herself, are mainly pasteboard, wearing labels instead of defining themselves through speech and gesture.

A notable element of the novel is its revelation of the author's social attitudes—that is, insofar as we can take Miss Marple as her mouthpiece. Miss Marple plainly believes the kind idealism expressed in the school's rehabilitation program for juvenile delinquents to be foolish and misdirected. She sees Lewis Serrocold, who runs the school, as a crank "bitten by the bug of wanting to improve everybody's lives for them. And really, you know, nobody can do that but yourself." As far as Miss Marple is concerned, "the young people with a good heredity, and brought up wisely in a good home and with grit and pluck and the ability to get on in life—well, they are really, when one comes down to it, the sort of people a country *needs*."[6]

A less central point, but one worth mentioning, is that Christie substitutes slurring remarks about Italians for the anti-Semitic comments that often occur in her novels of the 1930s. The change, of course, may indicate nothing other than differences in the habits of English speech. Whether such matters represent the writer's personal views or whether they represent the English as they talked remains uncertain.

The two 1953 detective stories, *A Pocket Full of Rye* and *After the Funeral,* or *Funerals Are Fatal,* again illustrate the basic difference in effect between novels featuring Miss Marple and those featuring Hercule Poirot. In both works, the murderer is a member of a diverse extended family, and in both the writer supplies surprise endings after lavish use of twists and turns. But in *A Pocket Full of Rye,* much of Miss Marple's deduction remains private until, bit by bit, she shares her insights with the policeman in charge of the case. In *After the Funeral,* Poirot shares key clues as he finds them.

The competitive reader may prefer *After the Funeral,* but one deduces that Agatha Christie may have had more fun writing *A Pocket Full of Rye*—mainly because some of her misdirection here involves reader assumption that she is repeating her formulas, when in fact she is reversing gambits she had used before. The title and the circumstances of three murders, for instance, set up another nursery rhyme formula until Miss Marple perceives that the pattern itself is meant to misdirect. Then, with several characters remarking at intervals on the general unlikeability of the whole household, Christie surprisingly makes one of her few attractive characters the murderer. She also plays games with the reader, providing flawed alibis for everybody but the murderer, with no real advance notice that he cannot be trusted.

A *Pocket Full of Rye* reuses a number of character types from earlier novels, including a surviving child of a partner the victim had cheated out of an African mine (*Hercule Poirot's Christmas*), a young second wife unfaithful to an old, rich husband (*Crooked House*), and an awkward adult daughter (*Murder Is Easy, Mrs. McGinty's Dead,* and *They Do It with Mirrors*).

In *After the Funeral*, Agatha Christie's self-repetitions are less particular, though as critic Anthony Boucher noted in the *New York Times,* the novel "is much more conventional than her recent successes—so much so that only topical references keep you from thinking that this is a revival of one of her novels of the mid-thirties."[7] Following the pattern of many early Christie novels, *After the Funeral* has a dominant man controlling the fortunes of a large diverse family, with many of his relatives greedy to inherit from him. The characters themselves are familiar Christie types, but the writer develops fine social satire, especially in a funeral scene and at a family gathering in which the survivors select mementos of the dead man.

The narrative, above all a puzzle story, offers plenty of suspects. As Poirot, focusing on motives, muses:

But it was not to be so easy.
    Because he could visualize almost all of these people as a possible—though not a probable—murderer. George might kill—as a cornered rat kills. Susan calmly—efficiently—to further a plan. Gregory because he had that queer morbid streak which discounts and invites, almost craves, punishment. Michael because he was ambitious and had a murderer's cock-sure vanity. Rosamund because she was frighteningly simple in outlook. Timothy because he had hated and resented his brother and had craved the power his brother's money would give. Maude because Timothy was her child and where her child was concerned she would be ruthless. Even Miss Gilchrist, he thought, might have comtemplated murder if it could have restored to her The Willow Tree in its ladylike glory![8]

All these suspects, Poirot discovers, have lied about whether they had opportunity to commit murder. Their dubious personality traits and flawed alibis make a thick smoke screen for verbal clues that point straight at the murderer. The reader should spot the guilty person, but probably won't, unless he pays attention to one character's chatter when no one seems to be listening, or another's surprise at what appears in a mirror.

In her 1955 detective novel, *Hickory Dickory Dock,* or *Hickory Dickory Death,* Agatha Christie experiments with a new kind of setting, a London hostel for students and other young people, run by the sister of Poirot's secretary, Miss Lemon. But in most elements of the narrative, the writer simply replays old tricks, perhaps less well than usual.

The nursery rhyme title, for example, is nearly extraneous. In fact, Christie makes more of the housekeeper's name, Mrs. Hubbard, and "Old Mother Hubbard" than of "Hickory, Dickory Dock." Further, for a Poirot novel, *Hickory Dickory Dock* has a surprising lack of subtlety in characterization, plot development, and resolution. For the most part, Poirot uncovers clues more in the style of Miss Marple than in his own. He senses hidden relationships and motives instead of deducing them from clues also available to the reader—unless that reader has a long memory for Christiean devices and can spot a switched-baggage gambit from "The Ambassador's Boots" (from the romance thriller *Partners in Crime*), stone switching from "The Case of the Distressed Lady" (*Parker Pyne Investigates*), or such staple Christie gimmicks as a false time of killing arranged by the murderer's accomplice, a faked suicide note, and a police investigator's rejecting the real murderer as a suspect.

The basic pattern of *Hickory Dickory Dock* is a system of layers. The narrative begins with a series of episodes of petty theft and petty vandalism, deepens into three instances of murder, and ends with revelation of characters' constitutional criminality. Christie finds ingenious ways to link her layers, but she fails to create a sense of logical necessity between events.

The 1956 *Dead Man's Folly,* has, like *Hickory Dickory Dock,* a better beginning than ending. The novel opens with fresh, amusing character sketches and a situation allowing dry, but gentle, social satire. But its resolution creates suspicion that the writer might no longer be planning the solution first, then meticulously working backward to plant real, as well as false, clues.

Set during a charity fete at a country house like the Mallowan's own Greenway House, the novel reports another Ariadne Oliver–Poirot collaboration. Mrs. Oliver involves Poirot, with the ostensible purpose of awarding prizes at a murder hunt she has arranged for the fete, but with the actual purpose of allaying her intuitive sense that something is wrong. The discovery that the thirteen-year-old who played the victim has actually been murdered justifies her unease.

The story begins as a variation on the closed-circle pattern. The fete itself attracts a horde of visitors, a youth hostel next door introduces an assortment of foreigners, and a mysterious cousin arrives on a yacht. But after amusing pictures of fete-givers and goers, and after due attention to Mrs. Oliver's dizzying invention of theories to explain the girl's death and Mrs. Oliver's own remarkable appearances, both the police and Poirot are stumped. Neither can discover who killed the girl or account for the disappearance of the estate owner's wife.

Poirot, of course, finds his answers in the final pages, after unraveling a number of suspects' irrelevant secrets. Indeed he is more artful at this than at explaining the multiple murders that have occurred by then. His real clues take shape when he reassesses Mrs. Oliver's plot, assuming that she had translated her sensitivity to atmosphere and personalities into her plan for the murder game. Fitting these suggestions against the cast of suspects, he deduces the murderer's identity. The deductions work, however, only because an interested, and implicated, party seems to accept them, and they presuppose two thoroughly incredible disguises worn for a matter of years.

The 1957 Christie offering, *4:50 from Paddington,* or *What Mrs. McGillicuddy Saw,* also begins with humorous observation of social behavior, develops with reworked ploys and complications, and ends with identification of the murderer, a surprise largely because the writer has not offered clues that point in that direction. In other words, the novel offers one more case of Miss Marple's special intuition.

The opening sketch of Mrs. McGillicuddy fussily reviewing her Christmas shopping and trying, futilely, to convince railroad employees that she really did see a murder being committed in a passing train neatly plays with polite common sense confronting the bizarre. The high point of the novel, this sketch establishes a leitmotif for the work: the contrast between social values and attitudes of the 1930s and those of the 1950s. Once Mrs. McGillicuddy has confided in Miss Marple, and once Miss Marple has enlisted the aid of a bright young woman who picks a suitable site for the disposal of a body, the writer makes an issue of the anachronism of the site, Rutherford Hall, a country house now surrounded by housing developments, home base for a tribe of mismatched relatives whose lives are no longer tied to it.

The family group, all standard Christie figures, includes the ill-tempered, reclusive head of the Crackenthorpe family; a pompous politician; a slick but unsuccessful businessman; a black-sheep artist; their mates; a spinster sister; a village doctor; and so on. Following her usual pattern, the writer invents some motive for murder in virtually every character, but she delays the resolution with a particularly brazen set of false identifications of the corpse. As often happens in Marple stories, one suspect the reader has been encouraged to settle upon gets poisoned. Another threatening character believed to be at a distance proves to have been on the scene, innocently on the scene, all along. Then Miss Marple discovers that the secret marriage of a hitherto unsuspected character was the real motive for the first killing. To trap the killer, Miss Marple resorts to another favorite Christie device—creating a situation in which an uncertain witness, namely Mrs. McGillicuddy, sees the killer in the same posture in which he committed murder and thereby becomes sure of his identity.

With *4:50 from Paddington,* Agatha Christie had begun treating World War II as a remote cause of social disruption. A wartime marriage in France had linked that novel to the war. In the 1958 *Ordeal by Innocence,* adoption of a group of children left homeless by the war provides a situation in which several characters become suspect because they live in milieus in which they were not born, that is, in which their relationships with others are unnatural.

Ordeal by Innocence, even in its title, makes a point upon which the writer always insisted: the evildoer must be identified to free the innocent of suspicion that will otherwise blight their lives.

As though determined to prove that she need not merely redeploy old devices to make new detective novels, Mrs. Christie developed a fresh basic situation for *Ordeal by Innocence.* One of the adopted children of the Argyle family, convicted of murdering his mother, dies in prison before the witness who can give him an alibi comes forward. The witness discovers too late that he could have proved Jacko Argyle innocent and tries to make amends by explaining the situation to the Argyle family—the victim's husband, the secretary he wants to marry, the other four children, and the housekeeper who helped rear the children. Dumbfounded to discover his news is unwelcome, he comes to understand that if Jacko, the family delinquent, was innocent, one of the others must be guilty. Pinning guilt on the right person may be impossible, but unless he is identified, no other member of the family can ever lead a normal life.

As a murder mystery, the novel offers an especially tricky problem in detection, not only because the murder occurred in the past, but also because all but one member of the family had opportunity to kill. Within the mystery frame, it offers a tautly defined study of stresses and guilt feelings inside the family, feelings generated by the adoptive mother. No deliberately wicked force like Mrs. Boynton of *Appointment with Death*, Mrs. Argyle smothered her children with her obsessive mother love, arousing deep love-hate feelings with her relentless efforts to do good for them—in the home she built on a place the locals call Viper Point. The nice problem in the novel lies in the evocation of "How sharper than a serpent's tooth it is / To have a thankless child." The novel suggests that to have a parent demanding more thanks than a child can give also jeopardizes human relationships.

The resolution entails adroitly engineered surprises, but these are surprises that may leave the reader rueful, for they could have been anticipated had the reader watched closely enough for clues.

During the pastwar years, as Agatha Christie got older and as she devoted more and more of her energies to drama, the quality of her detective novels became less predictable. One year brought a taut, vintage Christie; the next perhaps a work in which she kept her characterization up to the mark but settled for frankly careless structure.

Chapter Seven
The Last Novels
(1959–1972)

In the final period of her career, Agatha Christie became increasingly careless about details, but even toward the end of her life she produced several brilliant detective novels.

The 1959 *Cat among the Pigeons,* however, was not one of her best efforts. The work mixes elements of the political thriller with those of the detective story. Jewels missing after a coup in Ramat, a Near Eastern sheikdom, occasion murders at a girls' school in England. Set mostly at the school, the tale allows several arresting sketches of teachers and parents, exhibiting Christie's nice sense of comedy-of-manners speech and gesture.

The plot of the novel falls short of the characterization. Though sometimes highly praised,[1] this plot requires an exceptional tolerance for coincidence in its development, and exceptional patience with authorial fudging in its resolution. For instance, one murderer just happens to have a room next door to that of the sister of the English friend of the sheik of Ramat and happens to see a reflection of that friend hiding jewels in the handle of his niece's tennis racquet. Then, to keep the identity of the occupant of that room a puzzle, the writer reveals the remarkable point that several people attached to the school just happen to have been in Ramat at the time of the coup. Further, several vaguely defined international groups interested in the jewels all recognize the possiblity that the jewels are hidden somewhere at the school, even though only one group has reason to *know* they are there. To these developments Christie adds the detail that the mother of one student expresses surprise at seeing someone she recognizes from her days in the intelligence service, but the headmistress, diverted by the spectacle of another mother lurching drunkenly across the school grounds, fails to listen. The mother who spotted the secret agent takes off on a private bus tour of Anatolia, leaving Hercule Poirot to arrive independently at identification of the first murderer. The missing mother returns only in time to panic that murderer—

who is being lulled by Poirot's accusing the wrong person—into
shooting the second murderer. Indeed, the fact that there are two
murderers sets up most of the surprise of the resolution, for the reader
has been encouraged, even in Poirot's cryptic comments, to assume
there must be only one.

After *Cat among the Pigeons,* the 1961 *Pale Horse* comes as reassuring
evidence that the writer, entering her seventies, could still crank out
fine detective fiction.

The core idea for *The Pale Horse,* according to *An Autobiography,*
was a fifty-year-old memory of a pharmacist Christie had met in her
hospital training, a mild-appearing man who carried around a lump
of curare because it made him feel powerful (*AA,* 241). The murderer
of *The Pale Horse* uses thallium rather than curare, and the
writer substitutes greed for lust for power as the motive behind the
mass, apparently random, poisonings. Ten years after the work was
published, a second connection between real life and the novel came
to light. A murderer used thallium at least six times before he was
finally discovered when a forensic specialist reminded a Scotland Yard
detective of the Christie novel.[2]

Despite these connections, startling coincidence plays a large part
in *The Pale Horse.* But whereas happenstance had been necessary in
Cat among the Pigeons both for assembling the cast and for effecting
the resolution, in *The Pale Horse* Christie uses it only in setting up
her story, and then primarily in inventing circumstances to explain
why disparate people know of each other. Specifically, her nonseries
detective, historian Mark Easterbrook, happens to see one victim in a
coffee bar and happens to know several others. Further, he happens
to have a cousin who wants him to snare Mrs. Ariadne Oliver for a
village fete, and that village has a house called the Pale Horse. When
Mrs. Oliver so identifies the house, Easterbrook connects the place
with a strange comment from a frightened girl. Finding the house
occupied by three women who boast of their skill in witchcraft and
hint that they can kill at long distance, he tries to find out how.

The positive merits of the work include the graceful Christie self-
directed irony of Mrs. Oliver's complaints about the trade of writing
detective novels; the portrait of Mrs. Dane Cathorpe, the sternly
Christian wife of a vicar; and the whole pattern of characters saying
self-revealing things that from one point of view might be taken as
cases of a killer's cockiness, from another, as innocent confessions of
quirks.

The 1962 *Mirror Crack'd from Side to Side,* or *The Mirror Crack'd,* brings back Miss Marple, a Miss Marple dealing with advancing age and coming to terms with a St. Mary Mead that has tract development, a supermarket, and a film star and her entourage, instead of Colonel and Mrs. Bantry, in the manor house.

The strength of the novel lies in its engaging picture of villagers adjusting to changing times: village ladies agog over new bathrooms in Gossington Hall; Miss Marple learning to value her housekeeper's good nature and skills in cooking enough to overlook her casual approach to housecleaning; and Miss Marple setting out to explore the development, feeling like Columbus in a new world. But Miss Marple quickly experiences "her usual series of recognitions" of the people who live there. Suddenly, mothers with prams, "sinister-looking Teds," and over-developed fifteen-year-old girls look familiar to her. "The new world was the same as the old. The houses were different, . . . the clothes were different, but the human beings were the same as they had always been."[3] Christie emphasizes this point and claims the continuing legitimacy of her detective's methods with the novel's title, a line from Tennyson's "The Lady of Shallot," which links Miss Marple's—and Agatha Christie's—Victorian view of human nature to the new social scene. In labeling social changes as more cosmetic than real, the writer proposes that her detective's old assumptions and methods still apply.

The reader may spot the plot detail that identifies the murderer more quickly here than in most Christie novels, since it depends on a widely publicized bit of medical information, but the writer plays her tricks of misdirection with enough finesse to raise doubts about whether that detail might be included to fool, rather than to set up the resolution. She raises doubt about whether the first victim could be the intended victim; she stresses a frozen stare on the face of the film star to suggest that any character in her general line of vision might be a suspect; she confuses issues by planting a blackmailer in the household; and she assigns cryptic speeches and behavior patterns that might be evidence of murderous design to a number of characters.

In the next year's detective novel, the 1963 *Clocks,* Agatha Christie offers nondirection rather than misdirection. She combines a thriller and murder mystery with a romance between an intelligence agent and a prime suspect. The narrative begins with a secretary finding an unidentified man in the sitting room of a blind woman, to whose home the girl has been summoned but not, apparently, by the woman herself. The gimmick that accounts for the novel's title, four extra clocks in the blind woman's house, seems to be a significant clue.

Yet this clue actually leads nowhere. It produces only a tacked-on explanatory detail in the resolution, where the reader learns that the two story threads, though twisted around each other, were never really connected. The reader will remain puzzled over why Christie switches between the first-person narrative voice of the intelligence agent and a third-person voice, and he may well be bemused to discover that the only significant clues lay in the seemingly insignificant act of characters looking at one person and being reminded of another whose name does not come to mind.

The reader capable of ignoring such haphazard plotting might find amusement in some of the sketches of minor characters, especially in the neighbor's pair of rambunctious sons, in the precocious little girl with the broken leg, or in the dotty lady with many cats. For others, Hercule Poirot's assessments of British and American detective novelists could be a redeeming feature. Of special interest is Poirot's judgment of Mrs. Ariadne Oliver, the lady Agatha Christie always used when she wanted to laugh at herself. Poirot declares:

"I have read also," he said, "some of the early works of Mrs. Ariadne Oliver. She is by way of being a friend of mine, and of yours, I think. I do not wholly approve of her works, mind you. The happenings in them are highly improbable. The long arm of coincidence is far too freely employed. And, being young at the time, she was foolish enough to make her detective a Finn, and it is clear that she knows nothing about Finns or Finland except possibly the works of Sibelius. Still, she has an original habit of mind, she makes an occasional shrewd deduction, and of later years she has learnt a good deal about things which she did not know before. Police procedure, for instance. She is also now a little more reliable on the subject of firearms. What was even more needed, she has possibly acquired a solicitor or a barrister friend who has put her right on certain points of the law."[4]

With the 1964 *Caribbean Mystery*, Agatha Christie exhibited her own original habit of mind and controlled her employment of coincidence. One of the best of the Marple novels, *A Caribbean Mystery* is the only straight Christie detective novel with a direct sequel (*Nemesis*, 1971) and the only Marple novel set outside England.

Despite her using the fictive island of St. Honore as her scene, the author sticks to her standard English types in her characters. She offers a new mix of characters, but as individuals they seem familiar figures to a Christie reader: a retired major with endless stories about his experiences in the former colonies, three married couples covering up stresses in their relationships, a rich valetudinarian and his attendants, a canon with a dominant spinster sister, an indulgent old doctor, and so on. Even the one West Indian of any prominence in the narrative turns out to be a standard figure: a greedy, not very bright servant girl.

The practiced touch evident in the character types also appears in the plot. The writer redeploys devices that had already served her well, and she gets away with them again. For instance, the first victim's staring over Miss Marple's shoulder limits the number of suspects and gives the reader some indication of which clues he needs to watch for. Yet in this novel, as in *Appointment with Death, Death Comes at the End,* and *The Mirror Crack'd from Side to Side,* the writer misleads freely after she has offered such fair direction. Also, as in earlier novels, she keeps the story moving with a pattern of three murders, the second being that of a blackmailer who knew something about the first murder. Further, she fools the reader, as she often had before, by suppressing the fact that damning evidence applies to the murderer, not just to other suspects who are given more attention. Finally, the murderer proves to be the kind of person usually shown to be guilty in Christie novels, but one whom the reader has probably not considered because he seemed the most, not least, likely suspect.

The major attractions of the firmly plotted *Caribbean Mystery* may be its disclosure of varied personalities through revealing dialogue, and the particularly effective dramatic tension effected by contrasting Miss Marple's dithery conversation with her cold assessments of those with whom she talks. In this work, more than in any other Marple novel, the lady self-consciously weighs the advantages of her manner as a disguise, even considering how much a fool she sounds when she twitters or how effective certain Victorian gestures might be.

Though changes in social patterns never become a real issue in *A Caribbean Mystery,* the novel includes some pointed comment on shifts in literary tastes. As the novel begins, Miss Marple is trying, unsuccessfully, to read a modern novel her fond but patronizing nephew has sent her. She indulges in her own sly patronizing:

So difficult—all about such unpleasant people, doing such very odd things and not, apparently, even enjoying them. "Sex" as a word had not been much mentioned in Miss Marple's young days, but there had been plenty of it—not talked about so much—but enjoyed far more than nowadays, or so it seemed to her. Though usually labelled Sin, she couldn't help feeling that that was preferable to what it seemed to be nowadays—a kind of Duty.

Miss Marple reads a few paragraphs of the novel and concludes: "To have sex experience urged on you exactly as though it was an iron tonic! Poor young things."[5]

In the 1965 *At Bertram's Hotel,* as in *A Caribbean Mystery,* Miss Marple leaves her St. Mary Mead milieu for a vacation in a new place, thanks to the generosity of her nephew Raymond West. She views her fortnight in London at Bertram's Hotel—drawn apparently from Brown's Hotel at the corner of Dover and Albemarle Streets[6]—as a nostalgic trip through old memories, but in fact she encounters new breeds: fast-track socialites, race car drivers, spoiled adolescents, drug dealers, and so on.

The novel just qualifies as a murder mystery, for the murder does not occur until the end of chapter 20. Before that point, an elderly clergyman has disappeared and a celebrated Irish woman has avoided encountering the daughter she abandoned as a child. But the narrative has focused on Miss Marple's pleasure in, but uneasiness over, the hotel's atmosphere, its re-creation of upper-middle-class luxuries and indulgences of an earlier day. The writer not only introduces the murder mystery element late, but she tangles that story thread with one about a gang of criminals who smuggle, rob trains, switch license plates on cars, and impersonate various eminently respectable people at the scenes of crimes.

While the plot of *At Bertram's Hotel* suffers from the apparently pointless complications Agatha Christie usually permitted herself only in her romantic thrillers, the acrid judgments of Miss Marple and her new associate, Chief Inspector "Father" Davy, define an interestingly grim view of English life in the 1960s, a view that may explain why the writer was modifying the formulas that served her well in her vintage years as a writer of classic detective fiction. Her best novels had granted her detective figures, and indeed many of her characters, intimate knowledge of human types moving in firmly established social settings. Individuals from outside the settings might appear, or individuals within the settings might violate norms, but once the disruptive elements were identified and removed, the norms themselves were reaffirmed.

In *At Bertram's Hotel,* Miss Marple realizes that the appearances of old respectabilities and old securities are false and exploitive. She admits, "I learned (what I suppose I really knew already) that one can never go back, that one should not ever try to go back—that the essence of life is going forward."[7] But if she cannot return to the old assurances, she also recognizes that the new reality, as represented by the young, is crude, ruthless, and greedy. Significantly, of the characters in the novel, only Miss Marple and Inspector Davy, both anachronisms themselves, have a firm sense of responsibility, and though they determine to insist on justice in the closing lines of the novel, neither seems clear about how to go about it.

The 1966 *Third Girl* offers a similar disenchanted view of the times. Singularly humorless for a Hercule Poirot–Ariadne Oliver tale, the novel describes a London of stark, ugly buildings; unwashed, scruffy young women on drugs; and long-haired effete young men. The young, however, prove victims of their elders. Further, although the novel ends with a proposal of marriage, the couple plan to leave England for Australia, a disturbing variation on the author's customary restoration-of-order conclusion.

Moreover, *The Third Girl,* like *At Bertram's Hotel,* lacks the firm plotting of vintage Christie detective fiction. The reader is not involved in an affirmation of the primacy of reason and order by seeing how clues lead to the conclusion, for the writer substitutes complications for effective misdirection. Instead of clues, the reader finds Poirot repetitively expressing frustration over these complications, complaining that the parts do not fit together. In fact, many parts never do fit, and the writer never supplies adequate explanations for a number of details: Why is the title character duped into believing that she is a multiple murderess? Why does she fail to suspect that one person using a wig and makeup plays two roles in her life? How does the rescuer Poirot assigns to protect her happen to appear at the scene of a murder? And why do two conspirators bother to involve themselves in art frauds after they have successfully stolen a great fortune?

The 1967 *Endless Night,* similarly weak in plotting if viewed as detective fiction, might properly be treated with the Mary Westmacott novels, for like them, it deals with a love relationship in which one party gives everything and the other party takes. Yet the writer structures *Endless Night* with devices she invented for earlier detective fiction, borrowing one element of misdirection from *The Murder of*

Roger Ackroyd, some plot elements from the short story "The Case of the Caretaker," and much of the basic situation from *Death on the Nile.* Further, her narrative includes gothic touches, such as a gypsy's curse, and suggestions that the artistically sensitive temperament may be a mask for total egoism, both elements that figured prominently in her early short stories.

Though charitable critics and husband Max Mallowan admired *Endless Night* as a study of a psychotic killer,[8] the reader, discovering the killer's identity in the closing pages, may be more surprised than informed about psychosis. For most of the novel, the murderer's voice ingratiates with its breezy self-knowledge and shrewd, good-humored assessments of others. Ambiguous hints from other characters who know him well serve as semihidden clues, but hardly develop into analysis of a personality vacillating over a choice that will mark him fundamentally evil or good.

Approaching the age of eighty, Agatha Christie described herself to Francis Wyndham as a "sausage machine" who had to think of her next novel as soon as one was made and the string cut.[9] But the machine was finally slowing down. The writer had always husbanded themes and devices. She had always been willing to reuse them in fresh combinations. But toward the end of her career, her exceptional gift for smooth recombining began to fail.

In her 1969 *Hallowe'en Party,* she put the same basic kind of murderer used in *Endless Night* into a Poirot tale set in suburbia and featuring a set of unattractive children and their elders. Again her killer masks an essentially evil character with surface charm and artistic temperament. Again his evil corrupts infatuated accomplices into participating in his murders for gain, even as it destroys his victims. Again he himself loves none but one intended victim, but love does not stop his trying to kill.

The strong similarities between *Hallowe'en Party* and *Endless Night* are not fully apparent until one compares the resolutions of the two novels and discovers the terms in which both define evil. Evil in both works is a cancerous sort of social development, not discoverable until too late. But these novels suggest that evil may be a disease more common than it seemed in the Christie whodunits of the 1930s and 1940s. In these later works, as in most of her late novels, Christie suggests that criminal violence might be an ever-present risk, perhaps an inevitable problem.

In short, not even the presence of Mrs. Ariadne Oliver provides a genuinely light, comic tone in *Hallowe'en Party*. The Christiephile might regret the absence but be willing to settle for a well-designed puzzle. But there are also design flaws in the puzzle of *Hallowe'en Party*. For practical purposes, the writer links two separate narrative threads—one emerging from the children's party and one developing from events in a fairyland quarry garden. She replaces the principal figures of the first thread with other characters in the second. Poirot discovers the conspiracy that links them, but the plot remains convoluted, and the writer never attends to a number of loose ends.

The 1971 *Nemesis* exhibits similar loose plotting as Agatha Christie again fails to account for some of the characters' knowledge of events, timely appearances, and so on. Offered as a sequel to the 1964 *Caribbean Mystery, Nemesis* records Miss Marple's efforts to satisfy the bequest and behest of her old ally, Mr. Rafiel. The narrative actually sets up two puzzles. First Miss Marple must find out what the late Mr. Rafiel had wanted her to do: discover whether his ne'er-do-well son had actually committed the murder for which he has been convicted. Then she must learn the real killer's identity. The answer to the first puzzle, which has no real parallel in earlier Christie narratives, comes by way of Miss Marple's following clues prearranged by Mr. Rafiel, and this part of the novel develops reader interest mainly through Miss Marple's assessments of social types she encounters on a coach tour of English houses and gardens. She presents these in comedy-of-manners style, but they serve later as an assortment of suspects when Miss Marple begins inquiry into the explanation of the past murder. This plot pattern echoes the 1958 *Ordeal by Innocence*.

This second plot pattern, the discovery of the murderer's motives, links *Nemesis* to another kind of Christie formula, that of *Hercule Poirot's Christmas* and *The Mirror Crack'd from Side to Side*. As in these novels, the writer defines destructive human impulses by reference to Greek or Shakespearean tragedy or to Tennysonian poetry. In *Nemesis,* for example, Miss Marple intuits that the murderer has the temperament of a Clytemnestra, but only gradually comes to see that a homosexual impulse may be as strong and destructive as a heterosexual marriage relationship. Miss Marple also echoes a judgment characters in *The Pale Horse* had debated: the most frightening way to present the witches of *Macbeth* would be as ordinary old women. Such allusions do not, of course, transform Christiean formulaic detective

fiction into tragedy. They simply underscore Miss Marple's conviction, apparently held by Agatha Christie, that evil is an identifiable
force in particular individuals.

Though several works appeared later, including a Poirot novel and
a Marple novel written in the 1940s for posthumous publication, the
1972 *Elephants Can Remember* was the last straight detective novel
Agatha Christie wrote. Despite such slips in details as altering age
differences among characters or having characters exhibit knowledge
they had denied having, *Elephants Can Remember* demonstrates that she
could still whip up an engaging whodunit featuring Hercule Poirot
and Ariadne Oliver.

Her basic plot, as she goes to some lengths to remind us, had already served her before in *Five Little Pigs,* or *Murder in Retrospect,* another tale in which Poirot ensures a young girl's happiness by proving
that one parent had not killed another. In *Elephants Can Remember,* he
shares investigative interviews with Mrs. Oliver, but again he learns
the truth by patching together a number of flawed memories. His solution, a bit of shell game, uses a loophole in Ronald Knox's 1929
Ten Commandments of Detection, yet it is a solution built on clues
fairly offered to the reader, though imbedded in the discrepant memories of various interviewees.

In his puzzle solving, Poirot is basically the same kind of sleuth he
had been since the 1920 *Mysterious Affair at Styles,* but Ariadne Oliver, in her last appearance as Agatha Christie's ironic self-portrait,
copes desperately with an unreliable memory. The writer, in her
eighties, seems to have indulged in an additional bit of fun with two
background characters, both younger than the author herself. Julia
Carstairs, in her seventies, struggles in and out of chairs, fusses with
a hearing problem, and finds current dress most peculiar; Mrs. Mat-
cham, aged seventy or eighty, "a very old woman, with a wrinkled
face, humped shoulders, and a general arthritic appearance," also has
trouble remembering.

A list of sixty-one detective novels does not lend itself to brief assessment. Yet the quantity itself directs the questions one must ask
about her career. What accounts for her extraordinary appeal? Why,
by 1980 had her work, primarily her work in the detective novel,
sold over five hundred million copies? Why were her novels translated

into 103 languages? What are the chances the novels will keep finding readers?

The central fact of Agatha Christie's appeal lies, I suspect, in the quality of the novels emphasized in this review. She mastered a formula that produces predictable resolution at the same time it allows enormous variation in development. Unlike most novels of the twentieth century, novels constructed according to the classic detective novel formula appeal to a taste for tight, controlling plot, for story *as* story, for an imagined world that satisfies both because it seems complete and apprehendable in itself, and because it simplifies our perceptions of chaos in the real world.

Christie earned her readership by clearly understanding the difference between essential pattern and variations. For fifty years, she absolutely respected reader expectation of tidy resolution following a teasing game. Her practice shows how totally she understood the art of keeping a familiar game interesting with mutations and permutations of ploys. She recognized that the detective novel, like a chess game or a nice rubber of contract bridge, depends on a mutual understanding among players (or author and reader), that conventions reliably communicate, even as they entail multiple possibilities. She could and did repeat patterns again and again, making them seem new, extracting surprises from them, by making minor switches here and there. In short, her essential appeal lies in her artful manipulation of conventions.

Recently, fashionable explanations for the Christie phenomenon have focused on psychological and sociological qualities in her work. No doubt Ernest Mandel, for instance, makes an accurate point when he proposes that golden-age detective fiction satisfied subjective needs of many readers by performing "the objective function of reconciling the upset, bored and anxious individual member of the middle class with the inevitability of bourgeois society."[10] No doubt Stephen Knight tells us something significant when he defines the ideology behind Christie's novels in terms of their flattering the nonexpert reader's penchant for seeing simple orderly observation arrive at truth.[11]

Yet the appeal of Agatha Christie's detective fiction reaches well beyond middle-class British readers, well beyond those hungry to see their informal reasoning processes or their class identities justified.

Perhaps no single Christie detective novel quite warrants the lady's reputation, but the whole body of her work in the form demonstrates that she earned her place as a master storyteller. She absolutely mastered her formula and always had the imagination to keep varying her gimmicks so that her novels would sound fresh and different.

The extra claim of this storyteller is that she created a special kind of never-never land for her readers. Her form itself declared that her detective novels represented something other than chaotic reality. But, like William Faulkner, she makes her readers believe in a stylized, simplified, mythical society with which a reader can come to terms. Her country houses and villages especially become true, if not real. In fact, they possibly become truer for American and other foreign readers than they could ever have been for the British.

If nobody ever really believed that the English society she used as background could have harbored as many murderers as she drew, one at least wants to believe in the patterns of civility her nonmurdering characters practice.

Further, one does find himself convinced, rightly or not, that her pictures of the minutia of daily British life must be real in at least a general sense. Without ever offering detailed description of architecture, interior decoration, or even landscape, in the course of her half-century-long career, Christie recorded the solid-sounding little points: what people ate, how they dressed, how they moved from place to place, with what objects they surrounded themselves, how they managed their housekeeping problems. As Emma Lathen remarks: "That quick and unerring eye for the homely detail is worth volumes of social history. In *Styles* we start out with servants, with open fires, with bedroom candles. Little by little, the servants fade away, electric lights reach the bedroom, and central heating warms good and bad alike. No one, including *The Economist,* has tracked the shift of English household practice from labour-intensive to capital-intensive with such unobtrusive persistency."[12]

How long will this kind of writing find readers? How long have Fielding, Smollett, Dickens, Trollope lasted? How long will readers be drawn to deft storytelling, whether or not they subscribe to the particular persuasions and social views of authors? Evidence indicates that such writers tend to have impressive survival rates.

Chapter Eight
Romance Thrillers
and Spy Novels

Early in her career, Agatha Christie firmly distinguished her romance thrillers from her detective novels. In *An Autobiography,* she admitted a preference for thrillers because they were easier and more fun to produce than detective fiction (*AA,* 267).

In fact, however, the lines between her romance thriller/spy tales and her detective novels blur, and in grouping her novels for review of her career, I have, in several instances, arbitrarily classified novels that could fit into either category. For want of a better principle of division, I have been guided by central figures. Thus, because the other Poirot novels are plainly detective tales, I treat the doubtful case of *The Big Four* as a detective novel. Because the early Tommy-Tuppence tales are romance thrillers, I treat all the novels featuring the pair under this head.

The differences between detective novels and romance or spy thrillers is a matter of structure and of focus. In a detective novel, the whodunit question is always paramount. Detective novels stress the investigator's discovery of truth, with any adventures the characters might experience woven into revelation of that truth. When Agatha Christie introduces extraneous matters such as love interest into her detective novels, she makes this element a minor, tacked-on detail of her resolution, a device that serves merely to reinforce her celebration of order—the classic point of detective fiction. As she explained: "I myself always found the love interest a terrible bore in detective stories. Love, I felt, belonged to romantic stories. To force a love motif into what should be a scientific process went much against the grain" (*AA,* 246). Further, her detective novels, for all their stretching of plausibility with suspects and discoveries, generally demand only selective suspension of disbelief, usually about circumstances of crime and its discovery.

Her thrillers allow much freer development of coincidence, much looser connection between episodes, and much less realistic definition of social experience. Adventure can follow adventure with the loosest kind of connection or, indeed, explanation. National or personal loyalty tends to separate heroes and heroines from villains, and even when criminal activity initiates plot problems, blind chance and instinct, rather than systematic thought, promote protagonists' efforts to resolve problems. Moreover, instead of the kind of simplification implicit in crime stories, that in which guilt and innocence become clean, direct questions, romance and spy thrillers simplify political issues and power structures. In Christie's hands, these thrillers also celebrate the amateur over the experienced, trained professional. Her earlier efforts in this form especially suggest that Britain's security might safely be left to bright young things with a craving for adventure.

Christie published her first book-length exercise in the romance thriller form (and her second book) in 1922. *The Secret Adversary* introduces the yet unmarried Tommy and Tuppence, principals she would use in five novels and seventeen short stories. A pastiche of inventions, *The Secret Adversary* traces the final triumph of young love over a somewhat vaguely defined international intrigue, and includes such business as a scene on the sinking *Lusitania,* patches of dialogue apparently cribbed from P. G. Wodehouse, and self-conscious echoes of *Dr. Faustus*.

The novel has plot only in the sense that it ends with all the identities revealed. The writer connects episodes with wild coincidences, but both characters and situations belong so entirely to a never-never land that questions about logical, causal connections become largely irrelevant. The heroine, Prudence (nicknamed Tuppence) Cowley, meets an old friend, Tommy Beresford, and proposes that they both deal with the postwar job problem by becoming adventurers. Tuppence overhears a reference to a Jane Finn—who may or may not have survived the sinking of a liner—and on impulse she uses the name when a man responds to an advertisement she and Tommy have placed in the newspapers, an advertisement in which they indicate their availability for adventurous work. From this point forward, the pair are plunged into experiences with bizarre characters all given to conspiring, kidnapping, and making threats.

Agatha Christie eventually admitted that the novel began when she overheard a conversation about a Jane Fish, a name she thought too extraordinary to use, even in a narrative like *The Secret Adversary* (*AA,* 266). But in rejecting that name, she exercised atypical restraint in a work that seems more a beginner's novel than *The Mysterious Affair at Styles,* which in fact preceded it.

Aside from its loose structure, the novel has a silly central premise, namely, that international conspirators and professional intelligence officers and policemen can never match well-born young Englishmen in plotting or in countering plots. At the end of *The Secret Adversary,* Christie goes so far as to have the power-mad, Faustian villain explain the invincibility of such heroes and heroines. He exclaims to Tommy, "*You!* I might have known!" and concedes Tommy's plain, wholesome advantage. "He is not clever, but it is hard to blind his eyes to facts."[1]

No one who has read to the end of *The Secret Adversary* need complain about its uninhibited plot resolution. Earlier episodes will have led the reader to expect nothing else, as one coincidental discovery or escape follows another. Nonetheless, a reader trained by Mrs. Christie's later work may find the dialogue of the novel trying. Her protagonists favor "Old Bean" and "Old Thing" for personal address, but their language is less unconvincing than the writer's rendering of American speech. Her American millionaire delivers such comments as "Bully for you! Fancy you a menial. It just tickles me to death." Then he adds: "But say now, I don't like it, Miss Tuppence, I sure don't. You're just as plucky as they make 'em, but I wish you'd keep right out of this. These crooks we're up against would as soon croak a girl as a man any day."[2]

For her second thriller, the 1925 *Secret of Chimneys,* Agatha Christie produced a potboiler peopled with caricatures of international types: either criminals who commit murder, blackmail, and theft, or policemen from various countries who find themselves outclassed, not by Tommy and Tuppence, but by a set of even younger amateur detectives.

Most of the characters masquerade, and the unfolding of plot is as much a matter of discovering social identity as guilt in crime. For instance, one suspect emerges as the missing prince of Herzoslovakia; another as an American intelligence agent. A former queen appears as a servant, and an apparent policeman is unmasked as a master jewel thief who calls himself King Victor. The speech and attitudes invented for these characters match the identities Christie assigns them. But again she betrays strange notions about American speech. For instance, an American presented as an expert on first editions delivers such remarks as "I opine . . . that there is considerable mystery about this little dust up," and "These Central European nations beat the band. . . . It's kind of being rumored around that the deceased gentleman was a Royal Highness."[3]

Less peculiar in their dialect, her English characters behave remarkably. For instance, a lady discovering a body in her house invites a stranger at the door to dispose of it when he admits that he was educated at Eton and Oxford. An undersecretary of state babbles foolishly, and the Scotland Yard representative in the tale, Superintendent Battle, tolerantly accepts suppression of evidence, and movement of bodies, with the comment: "Well, you see . . . most of my work has been among these people. What they call the upper classes, I mean. You see, the majority of people are always wondering what the neighbors will think. But tramps and aristocrats don't— they just do the first thing that comes into their heads, and they don't bother to think what anyone thinks of them."[4]

The difficulty of distinguishing tramps from aristocrats, or aristocrats from tramps, generates much of the narrative business in the novel. And though the fairy tale/crime story may be a slender reed on which to hang an explanation of Agatha Christie's social assumptions, her key premise seems to be that the pre–World War I social order may yet reassert itself. Its representatives may be in disguise and they may appear inept. They may even be confused with usurpers. Yet they can emerge prepared to reaffirm and reestablish old values. Their strengths, in short, may be quiescent, but in times of need, inbred resources can and will assert themselves.

Despite the featherweight dialogue and sentimental social analysis of *The Secret of Chimneys,* the novel does demonstrate the Christie gift for narrative pace. Without witty dialogue, without credible characters, without plausibility in plot development, she keeps the tale moving—near the edge of humor, if never really funny.

In 1929, Agatha Christie wrote a sequel to *The Secret of Chimneys.* In *The Seven Dials Mystery,* seven characters from the earlier novel reappear. Chimneys, the house of the marquis of Caterham, again serves as a setting, and bright young things who chatter Wodehousese again outdetect a tolerant, reliable Superintendent Battle and foil conspiring villains.

For *The Seven Dials Mystery,* Christie invents a less exotic, more English cast than that of *The Secret of Chimneys,* and though she rarely treated self-made social types sympathetically, two of the more appealing figures in *The Seven Dials Mystery* are the couple renting

Chimneys, Sir Oswald Coote, a tycoon of humble origins, and his wife, Maria. The loose plot begins in a comedy-of-manners vein, with exchanges between Lady Maria and an intimidating Scottish gardener, and with horseplay among the Cootes' young houseguests. These guests amuse themselves by accumulating alarm clocks to wake an habitual late sleeper. Their joke fails because the sleeper has been murdered with chloral.

With this murder and then another for the young folk to solve, the author pays little more attention to probability than she had in her first thriller. Instead, she invents plenty of action and a resolution more surprising than plausible. Her twist depends on playing with reader expectation about secret societies, but Christie does not bother with advance preparation for her conclusion, nor does she check reader sympathy for the characters eventually unmasked as villains.

Though Agatha Christie wrote a collection of short stories, *Partners in Crime,* in 1929, and though she used elements of the romance thriller in several detective novels of the 1930s, she did not, strictly speaking, return to the form until 1941, with a Tommy-Tuppence spy tale, *N or M.?* Written simultaneously with the Miss Marple novel, *The Body in the Library, N or M.?* was a continuation of *The Secret Adversary,* but with Tommy and Tuppence old enough to have adult children (the twins with whom Tuppence was pregnant in 1929?) pursuing their own wartime lives.

While Agatha Christie's approach to plot in thriller writing had not changed much, she produced better dialogue and more cleverly defined background figures than she had before. In *N or M.?* Christie relies on gesture and turn of speech, rather than on description, to define personalities. Still, however, she treats thriller writing as a kind of holiday from detective fiction. There she might strain credulity from time to time, but a reader could expect to discover narrative purpose even in astonishing developments. In *N or M.?* she permits herself such unlikely business as a pointless twenty-mile hike for Tuppence. And, as in the earlier Beresford novel, she offers amateur muddling as an antidote to official bungling, and personal pluck as the answer to national political crisis. Yet the work has two interesting links to the detective novel *One, Two, Buckle My Shoe.* Like that novel, it warns against taking national loyalty for granted, and Tuppence, like Poirot, discovers truth by remembering a scriptural situation that parallels the case at hand.

Agatha Christie waited ten years before writing another thriller, but her 1951 *They Came to Baghdad* signaled a return to a conspiracy motif she had first used in the 1927 Poirot novel, *The Big Four.* It also began a new subgroup of conspiracy novels that would include the 1954 *Destination Unknown,* or *So Many Steps to Death;* the 1970 *Passenger to Frankfurt: An Extravaganza;* and, to a lesser extent, the 1973 *Postern of Fate.* This group lays greater stress on conspiracy than on love interest.

Like *The Big Four,* three of these novels turn on a discovery of sinister, extranational plots for world dominion, and traces of such activity in the past set up the plot of *Postern of Fate.* Three of the novels entail the buying of men of genius by ruthless individuals of incalculable wealth, and all four proclaim the value of ordinary, chaotic liberty over schemes for new worlds. In *The Big Four, Destination Unknown,* and *Passenger to Frankfurt,* plotters work from great manmade caves. In *They Came to Baghdad, Destination Unknown,* and *Passenger to Frankfurt,* the tools of the conspiracy are lured by simple egotism mixed with perverted idealism, while the ring leaders are motivated by naked hunger for power and money. All these novels allude to real geopolitical events, but the fictive conspirators do not align themselves with specific national interests.

Further, *They Came to Baghdad* and *Passenger to Frankfurt* are full of Wagnerian echoes. Both celebrate the power of love in something like a watered-down *Götterdämmerung* fashion. Both, indeed, include young men described as Siegfried figures. But these echoes raise more questions than they answer. Was Agatha Christie simply reworking a formula when she reused such allusions? Did her real interest in Wagner merely prompt echoes in narratives that, by definition, called for hints of monumental collisions of opposing forces? Or did these novels uncover grave anxieties about the threats posed to existing social orders by scientific developments and new concentrations of wealth?

Current events figure significantly in *They Came to Baghdad,* in which characters allude to the 1949 attempt to assassinate the Shah of Iran, the 1948 assassination of Count Folke Bernadotte, summit meetings between Western and Soviet leaders, and working arrangements between British and American intelligence services. Less specifically, the novel also makes much of currency restrictions for traveling Britons.

The setting, too, has a topical quality, for Agatha Christie dwells on Western influences on Baghdad, influences visible on the one hand in imposing modern architecture, on the other hand in sprawling shanty towns. Her most evocatively described scenes, however, are not those of Baghdad and Basra, but those of an archaeological dig site in the desert. In clean, spare prose she creates a haunting sense of life on Iraqi tells.

In her secondary characters, especially her archaeologists and other British expatriates, she proves herself as nice a social caricaturist as in her better detective novels of the period. With her compulsive liar of a central figure, Victoria Jones, she creates the most engaging of her plucky, adventurous heroines.

Despite its vivid setting and occasionally arresting characters, the novel has a plot requiring not merely willing, but eager, suspension of disbelief. This plot depends on extremely free use of coincidental meetings and on the success of a series of disguises and assumed identities. More fundamentally, it demands credence in an elaborate conspiracy of all world powers.

The 1954 *Destination Unknown*, or *So Many Steps to Death*, seems to have been developed from a detail of *They Came to Baghdad*. In *They Came to Baghdad*, the secret that had all the intelligence agents looking for one man, and that had occasioned several deaths, concerned the location of a mysterious hideaway of conspirators. In *Destination Unknown*, the key characters go to a similar hideaway and then try to escape from it. The two novels share several plot devices and details of setting. Both, for example, contain strikingly parallel accounts of plane trips with stewardesses who talk like nursery governesses, and both tales are set in Near Eastern deserts.

On the whole, *Destination Unknown* has far less convincing characters and a more extravagant plot than *They Came to Baghdad*. Missing scientists from around the world have been lured to a think tank, run much like a prison, and hidden in a leper hospital in the middle of a desert. The resolution consists first in the discovery of the hidden place by the authorities and then in the stripping away of character disguises and assumed identities.

The novel ends with several of the captive scientists escaping to their former lives and with one being charged with an earlier murder. The resolution suggests, but not very precisely, that the world has been temporarily saved from power grabbers.

For her 1968 *By the Pricking of My Thumbs*, Agatha Christie revived her adventuring couple, Tommy and Tuppence Beresford, now in their sixties, but still young in spirit, for a tale in which she fuses murder mystery, criminal gang smashing, and geriatric romancing.

The narrative opens with Tommy and Tuppence visiting Tommy's cantankerous old Aunt Ada at Sunny Ridge nursing home, where Tuppence becomes interested in an old lady who points at the fireplace and asks, "Was it your poor child?" The strange question haunts Tuppence, as it seems to have haunted the writer, who had already used it in *Sleeping Murder,* the Marple novel written in the 1940s and published in 1976, and also in the 1961 *Pale Horse.* When, after Aunt Ada's death, the Beresfords visit the nursing home again to deal with their relative's effects, Tuppence finds that her old lady has disappeared. Convinced that "the pricking of her thumbs" forebodes danger, Tuppence sets out to locate the old lady. Since the lady had given Aunt Ada a picture of a house by a canal that Tuppence remembered having seen from a train window, the search begins in an effort to find the house.

Though Christie creates strong characterizations and effective setting in the novel, she permits herself great latitude in plotting. For her chief ploy she reuses a gimmick that had already served her well—in *Peril at End House; One, Two, Buckle My Shoe; A Murder Is Announced; The Mirror Crack'd from Side to Side;* and *At Bertram's Hotel.* She misdirects the reader by encouraging him to see events from the wrong angle because the investigator begins by seeing them that way. In *By the Pricking of My Thumbs,* the ploy works less well than it had before, because Mrs. Christie involves herself in impossible chronological sequences. For instance, Mrs. Lancaster, Tuppence's old lady, is in her seventies when she disappears from the nursing home. She had, some twenty years earlier, lived in a village in which several children had been murdered. As a girl of around twenty, which would had to have been some fifty years in the past, she had been involved with a gang. But that gang, led by a man in his forties, is still active. Earl Bargainnier surmises that these chronological problems were due to the seventy-eight-year-old writer's having grown a bit careless with details.[5] Bargainnier may be right, but Agatha Christie had never practiced in thrillers the same order of meticulous planning she exercised in her detective novels.

A reader who can ignore these chronological problems may respond to the engaging character types invented for *By the Pricking of My Thumbs* and also, perhaps, to the tone, which is much like that of the

1961 *Pale Horse.* In both works, the writer creates a seemingly ordinary social surface, then imbues it with a sense of evil, which she exorcises in resolutions that provide matter-of-fact, this-worldly explanations for events.

In her introduction to the 1970 *Passenger to Frankfurt: An Extravaganza,* her eightieth-birthday publication, Agatha Christie insists that characters and plot in her writing had always been inventions—but that her settings, either in the narrow sense of place or in the broader sense of social atmosphere, always had been real. She proposes that increased violence, rebellion, drug use, attention to alienated youth, and general anarchy around the world indicate the reemergence of humanity's cyclical impulse to self-destruction.

> Can one envisage a fantastic cause? A secret Campaign for Power? Can a maniacal desire for destruction create a new world? Can one go a step further and suggest deliverance by fantastic and impossible-sounding means?
>
> Nothing is impossible; science has taught us that.
>
> This story is in essence a fantasy. It pretends to be nothing more.
>
> But most of the things that happen in it are happening or giving promise of happening in the world of today.
>
> It is not an impossible story—it is only a fantastic one.[6]

Christie biographer Janet Morgan quotes a 1966 notebook from the Mallowans' visit to the United States, which reveals the writer's first notes for the novel.

> Airport. Renata. . . . Sir Neil at War Office of M14. His obstinacy aroused. Puts advertisement in. . . . Hitler idea. Concealed in a lunatic asylum. One of many who think they are Napoleon—or Hitler—or Mussolini. One of them was smuggled out. H took his place. . . . Branded him on sole of foot—a swastika. The son. Born 1945. Now 24. In Argentine? USA? Rudi, the Young Siegfried.[7]

To these ideas Agatha Christie joined her earlier interest in the kind of character she created in Mrs. Boynton of *Murder in Mesopotamia:* "old lady Bertha Krupp—Armament heiress." Then she asked her publisher, Collins, for paperbacks of the writings of Marcuse, Fanon, and Chomsky, and from her research she culled expressions of current youth culture and anarchistic doctrine.[8]

The narrative she produced features a neo-Nazi movement centered in Austria and run by a grotesque old woman of vast wealth, who sits like a gross spider in the center of a web of subversive activities. She uses as a front a young man called either Franz Joseph or Siegfried, a young man believed to be Hitler's son, well trained as a spellbinding orator and skilled at taking his theatrical part in comic-opera sorts of rituals. The forces for good include Sir Stafford Nye, a man who never rose in diplomatic circles because of his ironic sense of humor; the Countess Renata Zerkowski—alias Mary Ann or Daphne Theodofanous—who bears so strong a physical resemblance to Nye that he suspects they must be distantly related; and a set of aging but loyal Britons, such as Nye's aunt, Lady Mathilda Cleckheaton, Mr. Robinson, from *Cat among the Pigeons* and *At Bertram's Hotel,* Colonel Pikeway, who had appeared in *Cat among the Pigeons* and who would play a role in *Postern of Fate,* Lord Edward Altamount who "stands for England," and Robert Shoreham, "one of the greatest geniuses of our age," who had discovered a drug called Benvo that made people permanently benevolent.

The body of the novel consists mainly of meetings among representatives of the opposing groups, those engaged in, and those opposing, the power conspiracy. Conversations rarely amount to more than vaunts from the forces of evil; and from the forces of good, either lamentations about disorder and menace around the world or expressions of desperate, but high, resolve to preserve civilized values.

In the end, forces of good get ahead of the game by discovering the identities of traitors in their own circle, but Christie adds a touch of traditional comic resolution with telegrams about marriage arrangements between Nye and Mary Ann.

Any summary of the narrative makes the novel sound like a political spoof, but the writer's tone is consistently grim and her manner is preachy. Nonetheless, the novel sold sensationally—in Janet Morgan's view because it dealt "with universal and timeless themes" and because Agatha Christie "had hit raw nerves."[9]

Though *Postern of Fate* repeats the idea that civilized values will fall under repeated siege by destructive elements that surface generation after generation, this 1973 novel turned out less a thriller than a garrulous, repetitive, careless mix of reminiscences and muddled details. For example, the writer fills pages with Tuppence's pleasure at finding favorite children's books in her recently acquired house. These books and the named toys that also delight the aging Tuppence match the books and toys the writer fondly recalled in *An Autobiography,* but there she described them with far greater economy. Christie also apostrophizes the Beresfords' Manchester terrier at great length, and the novel is marred by blatant inconsistencies: the Beresford's twin grandchildren become, within a few chapters, a group of three children ranging in age from eight to fifteen. Additionally, characters reminisce about their earlier career until they become tedious, talking again and again about their success in *N or M?*

The plot of *Postern of Fate* never develops clear shape. Tommy and Tuppence set out to discover why a child who later died had under-lined letters in a Robert Louis Stevenson book, spelling out his view that a woman did not die naturally. Two people are murdered, and Tuppence is shot and nearly poisoned, to prevent the couple's uncov-ering details of a crime that had occurred in 1914. In this crime, the villain masked a poisoning by feeding a number of people spinach mixed with foxglove leaves. Aside from chronological problems, of a piece with those in *By the Pricking of My Thumbs,* the clues never really add up. This problem becomes painfully evident when many of the characters gather at the end to admire Tuppence's cleverness—and she offers all the clues in a list.

Reportedly, Agatha Christie's daughter, Rosalind, fearful of her mother's literary reputation, asked her publishers not to press for more books after *Postern of Fate,*[10] and she wrote no more.

In all likelihood, Agatha Christie's thrillers never contributed greatly to her reputation. Her detective stories and novels were the works that drew and held her readers. When she admitted writing thrillers because they were less demanding and, therefore, more fun to do, she analyzed their essential character. One can read her detec-tive novels with some satisfaction even a second or third time, finding pleasure in her craftsmanship. The thrillers are readable only once. They are arguably more entertaining than the work of other practi-tioners of the form, such as Ian Fleming, especially for readers who do not crave blood and mayhem and gadgetry. But their superiority rests entirely on Christie's deploying, even when she writes only for fun, the skills at humorous characterization and effective setting she honed for the detective-novel trade. What the Christie thrillers dem-onstrate is the great value of her deft plotting. In her detective fiction she almost always plotted carefully. In her thrillers she scarcely bothered.

Chapter Nine
The Mary Westmacott Novels

Agatha Christie frankly described her romance thrillers as play. Toward the six straight novels she signed as Mary Westmacott, her attitude was more ambivalent.

At first she was a closet romantic novelist. In *An Autobiography* she recalls writing her first Westmacott novel, *Giant's Bread*, in 1930.

> It had been exciting, to begin with, to be writing books—partly because as I did not feel I was a real author, it was each time astonishing that I should be able to write books that were actually *published*. Now I wrote books as a matter of course. It was my business to do so. People would not only publish them—they would urge me to get on with writing them. But the eternal longing to do something that is not my proper job, was sure to unsettle me; in fact it would be a dull life if it didn't.
>
> What I wanted to do now was to write something other than a detective story. So, with rather guilty feeling, I enjoyed myself writing a straight novel called *Giant's Bread*. It was mainly about music, and betrayed here and there that I knew little about the subject from the technical point of view. It was well reviewed and sold reasonably for what it was thought to be: a "first novel." I used the name of Mary Westmacott, and nobody knew that it was written by me. I managed to keep that fact a secret for fifteen years. (*AA*, 465)

Christie always remained convinced that detective fiction was her proper job. But when her publishers saw fit to stage a celebration of her sixtieth birthday and her sixtieth book in 1950, she responded to the party invitation with mildly irascible pride. "Thank you for asking me to meet Agatha Christie. If you don't mind, I am bringing my old friend Mary Westmacott with me."[1]

The Westmacott novels could never have established the kind of reputation the writer earned with her detective fiction, nor did they ever attract comparable readership. Yet they represent interesting work, especially if read in conjunction with *An Autobiography*. In all six novels, Christie reveals her essentially romantic view of human relationships. In the first three, *Giant's Bread, Unfinished Portrait,* and

Absent in the Spring, she extensively uses the recollections of her own childhood and early womanhood recorded in *An Autobiography*.

Apart from heavy reliance on autobiographical material, the six Westmacott novels share various themes. All deal with the painful nature of love, inequality of love, possessiveness, and failure in human perception. All build toward crises of awareness in central characters, of themselves and of others. But in each, recognition comes too late to prevent unhappiness. Further, characters in all six perceive themselves and others one-dimensionally, according to emotional states and relationships. And in all six, Christie indicates complexity in personality either by having the character recognize feelings never before acknowledged or by having him realize that others do not see him as he sees himself.

Further, all the Westmacott novels share certain kinds of narrative method. In each, the central figure undergoes an experience that jolts him out of his customary attitudes and into a reassessment of himself and his relationships. In three of the six, an element of supernatural interference manifests itself. In five of the six, at least one character contemplates suicide. Four of the six are tightly structured by lines of action, and in the other two, the writer pulls her threads together with focus on the interconnections among a small group of major figures. Three of the six begin with retrospective chapters that lay out major themes, then fill in information that leads to the conclusion. All six have surprising twists in their resolutions.

The 1930 *Giant's Bread,* the longest and least disciplined of the six novels, deals with a web of issues: musical genius as a relentless fate; misaligned loves; the ongoing force of childhood fantasies and fears; the power of yearning for a specific place; the determining influence of hereditary traits on behavior patterns; and the nature of friendship.

The narrative traces the life of Vernon Deyre, a late-blooming musical genius, and Agatha Christie uses speculation about the meaning of *The Giant,* Vernon's opera, for a rather grandiose statement of her own themes. In the introductory section, a shrewd old man states the large issues of the novel when he responds to *The Giant*. In the opera's ending, a pigmy figure that had survived the ages of Stone and Iron and Machinery confronts another Glacial Age. The old man recognizes that the pigmy figure, not the Moloch of Machinery, is the Giant and speculates: "One wonders," he said, "what has gone to the making of a thing like the Giant? What produces it? What feeds it? Heredity shapes the instrument—environment polishes and rounds it off—sex wakens it. . . . But there's more than that. There's its food."[2] The food, he suspects, must be the flesh and blood of the genius himself, and that of other people, too.

Vernon has a double heritage. His father has a five-hundred-year-old name, and his mother's people are thoroughly nonintellectual business folk. The combination equips him with both aesthetic sensibility and drive.

Throughout the novel, Agatha Christie relies on similar simplifying formulas. The personalities of the principal characters, for example, are so firmly fixed from childhood that their youthful judgments of one another serve as reliable foreshadowings of adult development. Further, characters' choices are absolute either/or decisions. When the central figure links himself with first one companion, then another, the ties signify total, if temporary, ascendency of some element of his character.

The writer heightens the effect of this essentially romantic approach to human personality and issues by inventing melodramatic circumstances to signal changes in Vernon's choices. For instance, in his twenties he suddenly discovers music and begins to study obsessively. He falls instantly in love with Nell and marries her though he had been drawn to Kate, the singer so committed to furthering his career that she sacrifices her own voice to sing in his first attempt at opera. Nell, however, is so driven by her own need for security that she seduces him away from music. Later, reported killed in the war, Vernon suffers amnesia when he learns that Nell has remarried. Recognized by Kate and his childhood friend, the impressario Sebastian Levinne, who arrange psychiatric treatment till he recovers his memory, Vernon willingly plays Enoch Arden because Nell, installed at Vernon's ancestral home with a rich American husband, leads him to believe that she is expecting a child. Reunited with Kate, Vernon retreats to Russia to study. Then when his cousin has wrecked her life and lies dying in New York, Vernon must choose whether to save Kate or Nell, when the ship on which they rush to America begins to sink. He chooses Nell only to realize that he really loves Kate. Finally, he rejects Nell's last overtures in order to pursue his music.

Despite the extravagance of the plot, much of the narrative is apparently based on real experience. For Vernon's personality, Christie presumably drew on Roger Sacheverell Coke, a young pianist whose parents were friends of Agatha Christie's sister.[3] Although for Vernon's career she fantasized beyond real-life recognition, the important section on his childhood bears similarity to details about her own early life, especially her life of the imagination. In fact, the boy's imaginary companions and fears are practically an early version of information recorded in *An Autobiography*. Also, though the section hardly fits the rest of the portrait of Nell, that character's experiences as a hospital nurse during World War I correspond to the writer's recollections of her own career as V.A.D.

In her next Mary Westmacott novel, the 1934 *Unfinished Portrait,* Agatha Christie used autobiographical materials again and in more fundamental ways, discarding highly fanciful plotting and the heavy-handed symbolisms of *Giant's Bread*. Max Mallowan said of the work: "The book is not one of her best because, exceptionally, it is a blend of real people and events with imagination. Only the initiated can know how much actual history is contained therein, but in Celia we have more nearly than anywhere else a portrait of Agatha."[4]

The story of a suicidal young woman whose marriage has collapsed and whose child has died, the novel is filled with details that also appear in *An Autobiography,* such as the central figure's relationships with her mother and grandmother, her recurring nightmare about "the Gun Man," and traumatic episodes of a live butterfly's being pinned to a hat and the loss of a pet canary. The novel also traces the heroine's marriage to a young man whose conduct in most particulars matches that assigned to Archie Christie in *An Autobiography*.

That the author should use her straight novel to analyze, and perhaps to come to terms with, the experiences of her own life and her own character makes the novel poignant reading for those captivated by her detective-fiction celebrations of rational control of life. But at least one critic, Dorothy B. Hughes, contends that in the Westmacott novels Agatha Christie

is trying to fathom herself and those who were a part of her world. The stories are the revelations of a woman of perception, a woman who is searching human emotions to preserve and heighten moments which must be remembered. She is writing of men and women whose dreams bleed when pricked, who are not beset by the gods or the fates, but who are made bereft by human frailties and a wanton expenditure of the loving heart.[5]

Quite apart from autobiographical questions—that is, purely as a matter of fictive technique—*Unfinished Portrait* offers an interesting experiment in management of narrative voice. A third-person voice recounts the life of Celia, the central figure, a life that has led her to a settled intent to commit suicide. At intervals, in a first-person voice, a disabled painter who is listening to this account assesses Celia, the extent of her self-awareness, and the selectivity of her memories. As a literary device, these assessments control perspective of the character. If intrusive, they nonetheless usefully underscore the implications of Celia's own omissions and blind spots.

Granting the autobiographical element of the novel, these intrusions have a further ramification. They suggest, almost chillingly, a novelist consciously distancing herself from material gleaned from her own life, evaluating its psychological and literary implications. Then, in the closing lines of the novel, the writer transposes even her distanced evaluation into the stuff of fiction, when the listener-evaluator extends his maimed hand to the heroine, only to realize that his stump of a hand triggers responses of horror, relief, and deliverance, as Celia meets the symbol of her lifelong fear, the Gun Man, face to face.

At least the second best novel of the Westmacott narratives, *Unfinished Portrait* stands as one of the most revealing illustrations in modern fiction of how a novelist makes a novel out of personal experience.

Agatha Christie viewed her 1944 *Absent in the Spring* as her best Westmacott novel and the best novel she ever wrote. It was, she declared, "the one book that has satisfied me completely." She added that it was

the book that I had always wanted to write, that had been clear in my mind. It was the picture of a woman with a complete image of herself, of what she was, but about which she was completely mistaken. Through her own actions, her own feelings and thoughts, this would be revealed to the reader. She would be, as it were, continually *meeting herself,* not recognizing herself, but becoming increasingly uneasy. What brought about this revelation would be the fact that for the first time in her life she was *alone*—completely alone—for four or five days. (AA, 484)

Using as background a rest house in Mesopotamia where travelers might well be stranded and left to their own devices, Agatha Christie "wrote that book in three days flat," beginning with the first and last chapters. The book had, she said, been growing inside her for six or seven years and it had "just come clearly out of the mist." "Frightened of interruptions," she went straight through the book, feeling that she must get it down on paper (*AA,* 485).

Barring the writer's experience with Near Eastern deserts, *An Autobiography* offers no real clue to the sources of *Absent in the Spring.* The work's taut structure and sharply defined theme, indeed, suggest that the novel must be viewed as a meticulously planned and integrated work of the imagination rather than as a vehicle for personal memories.

The central figure, Joan Scudamore, encounters an acquaintance from school days at an isolated rest house. Their conversation reveals the main features of Joan's life and her smug view of herself as valued wife and mother. Making conventional small talk, Joan regrets never having time by herself to think. In neat, ironic foreshadowing, her friend warns her about the risks of self-analysis, but Joan remains totally unable to recognize them. When her car fails to arrive, she slips, step by graduated step, into uneasiness, then disturbance, then confrontation with bald truth about her relationships with her husband and each of her three children. After getting lost in the desert and expecting to die there, she resolves to deal openly and honestly with her family, for she is convinced that "she had met herself and recognized herself."

The resolves seem strengthened when Joan engages in uncharacteristically frank discussion with a Russian woman on the train home. The second conversation sets up a neat before-after balance with the first, and it underscores the ironies of the conclusion. For when Joan gets home she slides easily into her old style of conversation with her daughter in London, then with her husband. She insists that she is not alone, and her husband agrees that she has him but thinks: "You are alone and you always will be. But, please God, you'll never know it." The nice ambivalent point is that Joan *has* known it, but whether she has already forgotten it remains uncertain.

After the controlled intensity of *Absent in the Spring,* Agatha Christie returned in her 1947 *The Rose and the Yew Tree* to single-minded, almost possessed characters displayed in sometimes realistic, sometimes fantastic situations. Again the novelist deals with several love relationships, focusing on the inability of her characters to understand themselves or those they love. Again she introduces the story proper by telling its ending first, then tracing the developments that led to that ending.

Her title comes from T. S. Eliot's "Little Gidding," the last part of the *Four Quartets:* "The moment of the rose and the moment of the

yew-tree/Are of equal duration." The idea of equal duration applies
to several loves in the narrative: that of the fairy-tale lady of St. Loo,
Isabella; that of John Gabriel, the war hero son of a plumber, who
abandons his political ambitions to run away with Isabella and who,
having abused her, is metamorphosed into near-saintliness on discovering by her death that she loved him; that of the maimed narrator,
Norreys, who also loves Isabella but who, as his sister-in-law explains, has never really understood himself or anyone else.

Unlike the other Westmacott novels, *the Rose and the Yew Tree* has
a fairly full gallery of secondary figures characterized by the kinds of
tricks-of-manners Agatha Christie used in her detective fiction. Especially arresting characters include the narrator's perceptive sister-in-
law and artist brother; Lady St. Loo; a veterinarian's abused wife; and
a string of characters involved in Gabriel's campaign as a Conservative
candidate. The writer indulges in wit with these characters, but she
handles her main theme, the difficulty of distinguishing between love
and self-deception, somberly.

Christie herself liked *The Rose and the Yew Tree*. In *An Autobiography,* she suggested that its creation was a spiritual experience for her.

> A few years later I wrote another book of Mary Westmacott—called *The
> Rose and the Yew Tree*. It is one I can always read with great pleasure, though
> it was not an imperative, like *Absent in the Spring*. But there again, the idea
> behind the book had been with me a long time—in fact since about 1929.
> Just a sketchy picture that I knew would come to life one day.
>
> One wonders where these things come *from*—I mean the ones that are a
> must. Sometimes I think that is the moment one feels nearest to God, be-
> cause you have been allowed to feel a little of the joy of pure creation. You
> have been able to make something that is not yourself. You know a kinship
> with the almighty, as you might on a seventh day when you see that what
> you have made is good. (*AA,* 486)

Dorothy B. Hughes, who also likes *The Rose and the Yew Tree*, notes
that the novel actually retells the story of Beauty and the Beast. The
Beauty, Isabella, chooses the Beast, Gabriel, and love is completed
only by sacrifice.[6] Christie's combination of fairy-tale motif with her
own manner of economical storytelling undoubtedly makes a readable
novel, but it does require a taste for romantic resolution, and tolerance for characters who embody single strong emotions.

The 1952 *A Daughter's a Daughter* holds a unique position among
the Westmacott novels because it is an adaptation of an earlier literary

effort. According to Janet Morgan, in 1951, turning over old papers, the writer came across a play she had written at the end of the 1930s. In 1940, she had sent a copy to Basil Dean, then another to Peter Saunders, who held the rights to *The Hollow* and who would stage *The Mousetrap*. Slightly amended, the play was tried out in Bath, but it was never taken to London. Pressed by a representative of Rinehart, her American publisher, for another Westmacott novel, she turned her play into a novel.[7] Apparently no printed copies of the play still exist.

In the novel, Agatha Christie develops almost as tight a structure as that she used in *Absent in the Spring,* and again she offers a tidy, if slightly ambivalent, resolution. A mother chooses to sacrifice her own interests to those of her possessive daughter. As the daughter's interference makes her mother's life unhappy, the mother resentfully refuses to interfere when she recognizes that her daughter is making a disastrous marriage. The two find a reconciliation only in parting, as the daughter leaves to make a fresh start in Canada and the mother drops her assumed brittle gaiety.

The last Westmacott novel, the 1956 *Burden,* examines the destructive possibilities of love within a family. As a final twist, Christie has her central character recognize that being loved is a greater burden than her own sacrificial love for a sister had been, even though it had controlled her life.

The primary issues in the novel are not, in any direct way, religious, but Christie uses religious experiences to foreshadow key events in the lives of two major figures, the heroine and the evangelist toward whom she reaches in the closing pages. Examining the writer's notebooks for 1955 projects, Janet Morgan discovered an item that she proposes as the key to *The Burden.* It was the quotation, "What shall it profit a man if he gain the whole world and lose his own soul?" followed by the initials M. W.[8]

Melodramatic in plot development, though not in narrative manner, *The Burden* traces the lives of two sisters. The elder child, Laura, starved for parental affection, prays that her baby sister, Shirley, will die and makes an unsuccessful effort to kill her. But after Laura rescues the baby from a fire, she becomes fiercely protective toward her and, in fact, raises her. Shirley, perhaps driven to escape Laura's smothering mother-love, marries a self-indulgent, improvident philanderer, who is stricken by polio just as his wife decides to leave him for another. The sick man's abuse of his wife prompts Laura to allow him to take too many sleeping pills. Though Shirley marries the man she had loved, she becomes a drunk to assuage her grief over her first husband's death, and Laura, as self-imposed penance, runs an establishment for retarded children. The evangelist delivering articles that had belonged to Shirley—whose death may have been in part a suicide—sees Laura as the woman whose face had been part of his mystic experience before he took up evangelism. (Ms. Morgan proposes that Christie adapted the figure of this evangelist from an abandoned story about a child with second sight.)[9] He challenges her to escape the past and make a normal life, and the novel ends with an indication that she will try.

Dorothy B. Hughes has protested vehemently against the Westmacott novels being labeled "women's stuff," fiction suitable only for the specific sentimental audience implied by that label.[10] She argues that these novels failed to attract an audience because they were mishandled by their publishers. The critic makes a case.

Yet the publisher's methods of promotion cannot be the only reason the Westmacott novels have attracted little serious attention. The real explanation may be that, with the exception of *Absent in the Spring,* these novels fall between fashions in straight fiction. Their focus on people's lives of quiet desperation and sense of alienation smacks too much of the real world as currently perceived to satisfy hard-core romantics, and the writer's impulse for romantic fantasizing is too pat, too sentimental, for those who like their fiction toughminded.

Chapter Ten
Plays

Though Agatha Christie's novels constitute the solid basis for her reputation, one of her plays, *The Mousetrap,* now holds the indisputable international record for an unbroken run (over three decades), her play *Witness for the Prosecution* proved a great critical success, and for a period in 1954 she had three different plays—*The Mousetrap, Witness for the Prosecution,* and *Spider's Web*—running simultaneously in London's West End.

At least one critic, Robert Graves, a former neighbor of the Mallowans, predicted that her plays would outlast her novels. "Nobody," he wrote, "could promise Agatha immortality as a novelist. Her English is school-girlish, her situations for the most part artificial, her detail faulty. Nevertheless, the novels are sure-fire stage successes— on the stage, critical judgment is mercifully suspended—and she may well figure in future histories of the theatre."[1]

The Christie dramatic canon includes six plays that others adapted from her fiction (five from her novels, one from a short story), one play on which she collaborated with another in adapting, six she adapted herself (five from novels, one from a story), and seven (including one collection of three one-act plays and one expansion of a radio play script) she wrote for the stage. All except the 1937 *Akhnaton* (published in 1973) have been staged, at least for short runs; of the lot, however, only seven have had major American productions.[2]

The adaptations by others consist of the 1928 *Alibi,* adapted from *The Murder of Roger Ackroyd* by Michael Morton; the 1936 *Love from a Stranger,* adapted from the short story "Philomel Cottage" by Frank Vosper; the 1940 *Peril at End House,* adapted by Arnold Ridley; the 1949 *Murder at the Vicarage,* adapted by Moie Charles and Barbara Toy; and two adaptations by Leslie Darbon, both produced after Christie's death: *A Murder Is Announced* (1977) and *Cards on the Table* (1981). There may be some poetic justice in the fact that none of these adaptations garnered the critical acclaim or sustained the long runs of the most popular of the writer's own adaptations or original plays.

With the exceptions of *Akhnaton,* which is set in ancient Egypt and which deals with clashes in religious and moral systems, and *Verdict,* which though it involves a murder focuses on the issue of destructive love, the plays are whodunits with ingenious surprise endings. For the stage, as for the printed page, Agatha Christie created characters typed almost to the point of caricature. Her plots set up a series of false suspects. In the plays, she never offers her clues quite as fairly as on the printed page, but she generally achieves sufficient suspension of disbelief to make the resolutions at least momentarily adequate. Her form itself leads to fairly talky first acts, for the puzzles typically require complicated narration of circumstances, but she adroitly invents action and paces major developments in her plays.

Others' adaptations of her fiction follow her original plots more slavishly than do her own. When Christie revised a work for the stage, she made changes with panache, and she disliked the way others stuck too closely to the original books (*AA,* 456). When she adapted herself, she blithely eliminated her detectives altogether. In fact, she never moved Hercule Poirot or Miss Marple from the page to the stage. The only detective she ever kept for a stage adaptation was Superintendent Battle in *Towards Zero.*

Showing no more compunction about dropping some of her other characters than she showed about dropping detectives, Christie usually preserved only the general nature of her original puzzles and often redesigned her endings a bit. In *Witness for the Prosecution* and *Ten Little Niggers,* or *Ten Little Indians,* for example, she added fresh twists that significantly changed the endings.

Her modifications are nearly always accommodations to stage requirements —that is, adjustment to eliminate changes in setting, to put necessary narrative information into the form of dialogue, to keep bits of action and movement interspersed with talk. Her sense of the requirements of the stage undoubtedly best explains her elimination of Poirot and Marple in her adaptations. On the printed page, her detectives had leisure for assessments of suspects' motives and detailed explanations of puzzles. But such essentially ratiocinative activities hardly lend themselves to stage representation. In her adaptations, Christie first concentrated on developing episodes that defined a mystery, then let the characters caught up in the events realize the facts of their situation in remarkably fast moving final scenes.

Except for *Akhnaton,* Agatha Christie used the same dramatic methods in writing directly for the stage that she practiced in her adaptations. The very fact that she could transfer much of the dialogue from the fiction directly to the stage makes a telling point about her uses of speech in her novels and stories. She seems always to have thought of characters in terms of how they might talk. Consequently, internal evidence alone never clearly indicates whether Christie initially thought of a particular story thread for the stage or for her fiction. This stage quality warrants grouping her plays chronologically, rather than according to whether they were original or adaptations.

She assessed her first staged play, *Black Coffee*, which ran briefly in the West End in 1930, as "a conventional spy thriller, and although full of clichés . . . not, I think, at all bad" (*AA*, 421). She did not see the play on stage herself, for she was in Mesopotamia during its run.

The play develops the same basic plot as "The Submarine Plans," the short story reworked in "The Incredible Theft." In the play, as in both stories, a scientist keeps his top secret plans lying about in a house filled with guests whom he does not know. In all three versions, the deadly plans become secondary to development of complicated conflicts among characters, and the twists depend on the audience's, or readers', being misled about loyalties.

Agatha Christie reported that she never believed that her 1937 *Akhnaton* would be produced. It never has been, though it was published in 1973.

Tracing events of some seventeen years in eleven scenes, the play deals with the efforts of Akhnaton, predecessor of Tutankhaton, to turn Egypt from polytheism to worship of the sun and to convert a love of conquest to a cultivation of brotherly love and beauty. The attempt fails, as even the soldier Horemheb, Akhnaton's dearest friend, comes to regard the pharaoh as a madman.

Max Mallowan viewed *Akhanaton* as "Agatha's most beautiful and profound play . . . brilliant in its delineation of character, tense with drama."[3] Christie critic Charles Osborne suggests that the play may also be its author's comment on "the opposing forces of aggressions and appeasement in the 1930s, comment pointing, albeit ironically and sadly, to the folly of appeasement."[4] More simply, the play, like the Mary Westmacott novels, points to Christie's mild restiveness with formulaic detective fiction. She showed no inclination to abandon this kind of writing, but evidently she wanted occasional relief from it.

Sometime in the late 1930s, the writer took advantage of her two

main outlets for relief with a play she later made into the Westmacott
novel, A Daughter's a Daughter. She offered it to Basil Dean in 1940
and to Peter Saunders in 1950. Attributed to Mary Westmacott
rather than Agatha Christie, the play was tried out in Bath but never
in London.[5]

With her 1945 Ten Little Niggers, or Ten Little Indians, Christie
confessed being drawn to the idea of converting her novel to a play
by the very difficulty of the shift. In An Autobiography she wrote:

> I thought to myself it would be exciting to see if I could make it into a
> play. At first sight that seemed impossible, because no one would be left to
> tell the tale, so I would have to alter it to a certain extent. It seemed to me
> that I could make a perfectly good play of it by one modification of the origi-
> nal story. I must make two of the characters innocent, to be reunited at the
> end and come safe out of the ordeal. This would not be contrary to the spirit
> of the original nursery rhyme, since there is one version of "Ten Little Nig-
> ger Boys" which ends: "He got married and then there were none." (AA,
> 457)

Ten Little Indians has proved a special favorite with community theater groups because the taut plot develops its own momentum, the
lines themselves create decisive characterization, and each act has
stunning curtain lines.

In adapting Appointment with Death for the stage, Agatha Christie
left the basic plot line unaltered, but she built up comic characters
and played down the brooding tone she had developed in the novel.
The dramatic version clearly shows the ingenuity of the plot. But
without the somber atmosphere the writer generated with the setting,
and the slow revelation of psychological abnormalities in the original
version, neither the characters nor the situation quite convince.

Neither Appointment with Death nor the 1946 adaptation of Death
on the Nile, Murder on the Nile (changed to Hidden Horizons for the
American production), was very well received.[6] The Times (London)
reviewer summarily dismissed the latter: "Once more the 'Who did
it?' piece, and this time in almost its crudest form."[7]

The 1951 Hollow fared better with its reviewer, who praised the
"effect of genuine surprise" of the ending.[8] In the dramatic version,
the characters still exhibit a certain stylized improbability as they had
in the novel. They represent social stereotypes rather than flesh and
blood. But the writer dances her elaborately costumed puppets vigor-
ously around the stage and finds ways to present the circumstantial

evidence against each until the real killer explains the murder at the end.

Not even Peter Saunders, its producer, seems to have been quite sure why the 1952 *Mousetrap* became the longest running play on record. "It will one day come off for no other reason than business suddenly collapses. And I shall no more be able to give a reason than I can now give one for its unprecedented success."[9] Nor did Agatha Christie understand the phenomenal success of the play. When it had run only thirteen years, she commented: "I must say it seems to me incredible. Why should a pleasant, enjoyable evening's play go on for *thirteen years*. No doubt about it, miracles happen" (*AA*, 500). The miracle, of course, had not then run half its course.

According to Janet Morgan, Agatha Christie formulated the idea that served first for "Three Blind Mice," a thirty-minute radio play in honor of the Queen Mother's eightieth birthday, on reading about the death of a young boy maltreated by foster parents.[10] Yet in explaining how she expanded her radio play, the writer identified a basic strength of her "pleasant, enjoyable evening's play":

The more I thought of *Three Blind Mice,* the more I felt that it might expand from a radio play lasting twenty minutes to a three-act thriller. It wanted a couple of extra characters, a fuller background and plot, and a slow working up to the climax. I think one of the advantages *The Mousetrap,* as the stage version of *Three Blind Mice* was called, has had over other plays is the fact that it was really written from a precis, so that it had to be the bare bones of the skeleton coated with flesh. It was all there in proportion from the first. That made for good construction. (*AA*, 498)

The elements of good construction in the play include eight arresting characters trapped by a blizzard in a guest house run by two young amateurs. One of those trapped, Sergeant Trotter, advises the others that one of their number is a murderer looking for his next victim. Circumstantial evidence emerges against every character, and qualities that seem merely comic from one point of view begin to look sinister from another. A pattern of shifting relationships keeps the characters themselves considering and reconsidering one another as suspects. Tensions within the play build steadily to a shattering finale, followed by a few lines of warmly comic readjustment.

With her 1953 *Witness for the Prosecution,* Agatha Christie offered another well-constructed play, though she worked from her 1948 short story "The Witness for the Prosecution." Although the work was her favorite among her plays, Christie admitted that she had not wanted to write it. Peter Saunders, after trying a first draft of adaptation himself, persuaded her to do it and cajoled her into reading up on trials in order to create the court scene. She wrote the play quickly, taking no more than two or three weeks after she had done her preparatory reading, and then stubbornly held out for an ending different from that of the short story version. "I got my end, and it was successful. Some people said it was a double cross, or dragged in, but I knew it wasn't: it was logical. It was what could have happened, what might have happened, and in my view probably would have happened—possibly with less violence, but the psychology would have been right, and the one little fact that lay beneath it had been implicit all through the play" (*AA*, 503). These comments reveal the core of the Christie method, as did her comment on the good construction of *The Mousetrap;* she tried for a logical explanation, implicit from the beginning though her audience may not have seen it, and for an explanation she saw as psychologically sound. Psychological soundness, in this instance, evidently refers to the motivation for the last, stark bit of business, but unmistakably the new ending also tidied up a problem of retributive justice. A notable characteristic of Christie's stage adaptations was always movement toward clarification of the point that murderers will be caught.

According to Charles Osborne, the play ran for 468 performances in its first London production, then for 646 in New York, where it won the New York Drama Critics Circle award for the best foreign play of 1954.[11] *Witness for the Prosecution* proved an extremely expensive play to produce, because it requires a cast of thirty (though the author proposed a system of doubling roles for repertory companies) and because it has two alternating sets including a replica of the Old Bailey. Its instant success justified the faith of Saunders, who had invested all his capital in it. The play also provided Agatha Christie with the only first night she confessed enjoying (*AA*, 501).

With *Spider's Web* in 1954, Christie created her only play written for a particular actress, Margaret Lockwood, whom she found enchanting in the comic lead (*AA*, 506).

Although the action centers on a strange body that appears in a drawing room, the mystery element is always secondary to comic business: characters are altogether matter-of-fact about bizarre developments; and there are running spoofs of standard detective-fiction gambits, such as mysterious passageways, obtuse police officers, disappearing bodies, and blundering alibis. Christie supplies her customary twist in the ending, but her plot is more sassy game than complex puzzler.

In spite of her resolve in 1945 to do future dramatic adaptations of her work herself, *Towards Zero,* produced in 1956, apparently incorporates the efforts of Gerald Verner as well as her own work. The extent of his contribution, elicited not by Christie herself, but by her American agent, Lee Shubert, remains uncertain. She had begun her own adaptation in 1943; Shubert had reviewed it in 1944 and proposed alterations. By 1950, the author, looking over the dramatized version, reported to her publisher that "the Whodunit with everyone suspected in turn, and plenty of comic red herrings thrown in, really by now quite sickens me on the stage." She added: "Frankly, I have never seen *Towards Zero* as good material for a play . . . its point is *not* suspicion of everybody—but suspicion and everything pointing toward the incrimination of *one* person—and rescue of that victim at the moment when she seems to be hopelessly doomed. But, if fun and thrills are wanted, go to some other of my fifty offspring!"[12]

The author's instincts about *Towards Zero* as a play were justified— it only ran for some six months. While the adaptation shows only the bare outline of the novel, with the flourishes of development and theme cut away, and while the shifts in several characters' functions reflect great ingenuity, the complexities of the plot do not lend themselves to stage development, even with a new final twist. Christie artfully plants her clues in dialogue, but in the denunciation scene she leaves explanation of characters' motives for bald announcement by the individuals themselves or by others.

For her 1958 *Verdict,* a two-act play that ran only one month, Agatha Christie has a murder occurring in full view. Instead of a mystery, the point, she explained, is that "an idealist is always dangerous, a possible destroyer of those who love him." She saw the play posing "the question of how far you can sacrifice, not yourself, but those you love, to what you believe in, even though they do not" (*AA,* 506). In other words, the play addresses the kind of theme Christie examines in her Mary Westmacott novels.

As in those novels, the characters are less convincing as humans than as embodiments of intense emotional states. The line of action unswervingly illustrates her message. For example, the idealist/ destroyer of the play, a professor Karl Hendryk, has made his invalid wife unhappy by defending others at the cost of his job and homeland. The wife's complaints make this point, but the professor continues the sacrifice. He accepts his student's stealing a valuable book and selling it for a pittance. Then he agrees to tutor a spoiled rich girl whose father buys his services by promising a possible cure for the wife. When the daughter poisons the wife in an attempt to seduce the professor, the professor allows his wife's cousin, who has long loved him, to be arrested and charged with the murder. As the play closes, the cousin, who has been acquitted, declares that she will be sacrificed no longer, but having vowed to go, she stays after all.

The affirmative ending rather compromises the point the writer herself defined. But according to Charles Osborne, the opening night audience booed when, because of a stagehand error, the play ended without her decision to stay. They applauded the more affirmative ending on the following night.[13] The applause did not, apparently, last long enough. In *An Autobiography,* Christie staunchly defended her work. "Later I was to write a play called *The Unexpected Guest,* and another which, though not a success with the public, satisfied me completely. It was put on under the title of *Verdict*—a bad title. I had called it *No Fields of Amaranth*" (*AA,* 506).

Despite the short run of *Verdict,* Agatha Christie quickly wrote another two-act play, *The Unexpected Guest,* which opened some two months after *Verdict.* As the play begins, it seems, like *Verdict,* to have little element of mystery, for the woman standing over the body of her husband admits that she has killed him. But as the action develops, many others are shown to have motives for murdering Richard Warwick, a psychopathic, crippled former big-game hunter. In the past, Warwick has run over children, amused himself by shooting at cats, bullied his retarded younger brother, harassed his aging mother, and abused his wife. When a stranger impulsively tries to shield the wife, his efforts cause delays that allow the audience to see how much the dead man has poisoned the lives of others and to consider circumstantial evidence against a range of characters, including a blackmailing servant, a housekeeper ready to protect the mentally deficient brother, and the wife's weak admirer, who is ready to let her take blame for the murder.

A grim little thriller, with virtually no comic touches, the play exhibits taut construction and exceptionally effective management of shifting suspicion, as each new development qualifies appearances. Further, the play has an uncommonly chilling curtain line.

In the 1960 *Go Back for Murder,* Agatha Christie tried an even trickier adaptation. Based on *Five Little Pigs,* or *Murder in Retrospect,* and preserving the main lines of the original plot and characterization, the play calls for quick changes in makeup and costume, as the first act is set in the present, the first half of the second act takes place sixteen years earlier, and the act ends back in the present.

The three one-act plays grouped for the 1962 *Rule of Three* ran for only ninety-two performances in London, and critics were unenthusiastic,[14] but the plays are firmly designed and nicely varied in tone. *The Rats* is pure thriller, a little episode in which two of the principals are lured into a flat. Locked in, and discovering a body in a chest, they turn on one another, and each reveals his ruthless egotism.

Afternoon at the Seaside, with basically the same plot as "The Rajah's Emerald" from the 1934 *Listerdale Mystery,* involves lower-middleclass holidayers on a beach. Business over a stolen necklace ties together generally satiric episodes of flirtations, petty snobberies, and games with speech patterns.

The Patient, another thriller, sets up the strongest twist ending of the three and further involves an interesting gimmick. The victim of an attempted murder lies heavily bandaged on a gurney on stage, while a physician explains to the several suspects that his experimental treatment may enable her to speak, thus revealing who pushed her off a balcony. The first phase of the experiment supplies the initial B, which applies to several suspects. Then, as suspects quarrel, they betray one another's motives until the play ends with a sharp surprise.

Agatha Christie's last play, the 1972 *Fiddler's Three,* was never staged in London. Initially called *Fiddler's Five,* the play was performed a few times in the provinces but is not, apparently, available in print.[15]

Agatha Christie's status as a playwright is analogous to her standing as a novelist and short story writer. She demands respect because a very large, discerning public has accorded her its attention. Other dramatists may have offered greater intellectual challenge or created more provocative plays. She made a frankly formulaic pattern uncommonly entertaining because she handled it with extraordinary finesse. Others may have written more innovative plays; she staked her claims on a modest kind of entertainment and exhibited the strength of real craftsmanship.

One sympathetic critic, J. C. Trewin, trying to analyze her success, concludes that its base must be her ability to set up an interesting problem and offer a quick, surprising solution to it. The effectiveness of her plays cannot entirely be explained in terms of her characters, whom Trewin describes as "attendants on a body" who "rarely had life of their own."[16]

In the end, perhaps, one accounts for *The Mousetrap* or *Witness for the Prosecution* or *Spider's Web* by simply granting that Agatha Christie understood audiences as she understood readers. She knew exactly how much both wanted first to be teased, then satisfied. She understood perfectly that a good riddle is nearly irresistible.

Chapter Eleven
Autobiographical Writing

Agatha Christie wrote two autobiographical books. In 1946 she published *Come, Tell Me How You Live*, a reminiscence of daily life on archaeological digs in Syria in the prewar years. Written in the early forties, it was signed Agatha Christie Mallowan. *An Autobiography*, finished in 1965, was posthumously published in 1977, and for this work she used her customary pen name, Agatha Christie.

In both quietly disarming works, the author makes no pretense of offering full diary or journal records of her life. In both, she confesses that she shares memories selectively, and in both she creates an unobtrusive literary persona for her self-portrait. On occasion, she exhibits a detached sort of interest in her own feelings and responses, but in the main, she concentrates less on explaining herself directly than on evoking the flavor of times and places and particular people in her life. In short, Christie's persona is primarily an organizing narrative device, and she shapes her material with other literary devices, such as measured recurrences of parallel episodes and references.

In the foreword to *Come, Tell Me How You Live*, dedicated to her husband and other members of the Mallowan digs, the writer announces: "A final warning so that there will be no disappointment. This is not a profound book—it will give you no interesting sidelights on archaeology, there will be no beautiful descriptions of scenery, no treating of economic problems, no racial reflections, no history. It is, in fact, small beer—a very little book, full of everyday doings and happenings."[1]

Come, Tell Me How You Live contains little direct information about Agatha Christie as a writer, only miscellaneous details such as the source of the name Shaitana in *Cards on the Table* and a description of a house at a dig that served as the model for the house in *Murder in Mesopotamia*. Instead of her own professional work, she focuses on a period of her private life as the wife of an archaeologist. Yet the "I" of the work is a persona who moves among firmly controlled roles.

At the beginning, and at intervals later, Agatha Christie plays the part of a baffled butt of outlandish situations. Her efforts to outfit herself for the excursion to the Middle East, for instance, lead her through a series of frustrating encounters with salespeople. She shapes the whole experience into a comedy that reaches a climax when a salesgirl asks her to agree that it would be unsuitable for the cruise department to carry outsizes.

Later, more experienced with digs, and traveling alone across Turkey to join her husband, she finds herself with two Turkish women, one of whom will share a compartment with her. Told of her companion's offspring and miscarriages, Christie tries to rise to the occasion. "I feel that for English prestige I cannot admit to being perfectly contented with one daughter. I add a couple of sons with shameless mendacity" (*Live,* 122).

In another role, the "I" of the narrative treats herself as the embodiment of English attitudes and experiences who confronts astonishing cultural differences. She plays this role in her report of being shown a hotel room already occupied by four sleepers, in her response to being asked for medical advice and learning that a sheik would probably dawdle until his senior wife died of blood poisoning, and in her rueful account of doomed efforts to get Arabic servants to practice English methods of dishwashing, table setting, and cooking. Her response to a servant's scheme for saving money by hiring an old woman, instead of buying a horse, to haul water fits into the same category, as do her report of the postman's determined effort to get the Mallowan party to accept all leftover mail addressed to Westerners and her tale of the worker who bargained with a dentist to pull four teeth instead of one, to make the price good.

The third role established for the narrator in *Come, Tell Me How You Live* is that of a raconteur who fondly recalls amusing experiences, such as her conviction that she has contracted some mysterious disease when she begins listing to the left and her subsequent discovery that her habit of reconnoitering dig sites by always moving counterclockwise has caused her shoes to wear down on only one side. She strikes the same note in her account of Max Mallowan's book packing and in reports of his happy absorption in his digging, absorption so complete that it leads him to describe his wife's clothing in terms of pottery patterns.

Apart from the development of an identifiably literary persona, the writer utilizes several structural devices in *Come, Tell Me How You Live* that separate her narrative from ordinary diary form. For example, she uses artfully arranged echoes. Fairly early in the narrative she tells the story of the Mallowans' returning to their house at Chagar with two French nuns and a French officer and finding a lavatory seat set proudly before their front door. The writer returns to the lavatory seat motif late in her narrative, when she describes how her mood of romantic farewell to the Middle East is shattered when a cargo ship crane drops a crate of lavatory seats, which float all over the harbor at Beirut.

Similarly, she organizes her narrative with nicely paced recurring references to English perceptions of the Middle East as the Holy Land. She first raises the point when describing the difficulties of explaining the dig site to acquaintances. Later, mulling over the stories of Jezebel and the Good Samaritan, she remarks on her fascinating discovery of the applicability of scriptural stories "couched in the language and ideology which we hear daily all around us." She adds, "I am often struck by the way the emphasis sometimes shifts from what one has commonly accepted" (*Live*, 179). Toward the end of the book, she reports her startling recognition of the similarity between the fanatically religious brothel-keeper and the biblical Rehab, the harlot.

Christie practices yet another kind of literary structuring with the attitudes of her persona. At the beginning of the narrative, the "I" tends to be shocked at Arab attitudes and codes of behavior. At the end, she is almost as amused as the Arabs at a newly arrived Englishman's distress over native attitudes toward pain and death.

Christie practices a still subtler organizing device with her title phrase, "Come, tell me how you live." Clearly, in the opening of her narrative, she is referring to explanations of how archaeologists manage their lives, and also to the subject of their inquiries, how ancient peoples lived. At the end of the book she speaks of archaeological camp life as "a very happy way to live," but her reference seems also to apply to the life-style of the Arabic workers she had come to know and admire. She closes her epilogue with a prayer. "Inshallah, I shall go there again, and the things that I love shall not have perished from this earth" (*Live*, 222).

An Autobiography is, by its very nature, larger in scope than *Come, Tell Me How You Live*, but the two books have much in common in method and tone.

In *An Autobiography*, Agatha Christie obviously recognizes that her readers will be primarily those who know her fiction, especially her detective novels, people interested in her reading and writing habits.

But she also uses *An Autobiography* for consciously selective personal self-analysis. As she explains in her foreword, autobiography is too grand a word for her intent. "It implies names, dates and places in tidy chronological order. What I want is to plunge my hand into a lucky dip and come up with a handful of assorted memories." She views the past as "the memories and realities that are the bedrock of one's present life" and defends her efforts to recapture moments of her own past. "We never know the whole man, though sometimes, in quick flashes, we know the true man. I think, myself, that one's memories represent those moments which, insignificant as they may seem, nevertheless represent the inner self and oneself as most really oneself" (*AA,* xiii). Later she confesses: "I have remembered, I suppose, what I wanted to remember; many ridiculous things for no reason that makes sense. That is the way we human creatures are" (*AA,* 510).

Christie rarely generalizes about what her own memories suggest about her inner self. She writes as a novelist, as one content to define a situation vividly and then let the reader abstract meanings. But in one exceptional passage she offers revealing comment on the progress of self-knowledge. She closes the chapter on her own earliest childhood memories with an anecdote about her grandson, Mathew, whom she observed muttering to himself, "This is Mathew going downstairs." His performance, she remarks, illustrates a stage of life in which we see, rather than feel, ourselves. The next stage, she adds, happens when it is "I" going down stairs, for the achievement of "I" is "the first step in the progress of a personal life" (*AA,* 52–53).

In tracing the progress of her own life, Agatha Christie practices selective candor. She describes some kinds of memories in devastating exactness, especially recollections of childhood pleasures and anxieties. She laces her narrative with sharply etched impressions, favorable and otherwise, of people who crossed her path. She plainly reveals her relish for their eccentricities, and she unsentimentally assesses their personalities. But she also practices Victorian reticence. She avoids mentioning her own birth date or those of her sister, brother, or daughter. This habit, however, may not be entirely a matter of literary method, for her biographer Gwen Robyns notes that she habitually drew veils over personal information, even that which is normally part of the public record. Her birth certificate, for example, turned up, not in Somerset House in London, the predictable place for such a thing, but in the office of the registrar of births, deaths, and marriages in Newton Abbot, a small town in Devon. Further, her mother's name did not appear on her marriage certificate to Archibald Christie, and it was misspelled on her marriage certificate to Max Mallowan. Also, both she and Mallowan misrepresented their ages on that record.[2]

In *An Autobiography*, Christie entirely ignores the most highly publicized episode of her eleven-day disappearance in 1926, shortly before the dissolution of her first marriage. Though she does discuss her pain and surprise over her divorce from Archie Christie, she passes over the specific details of the episode with seemly haste. Yet she produces pointed, by no means sentimental, sketches of relatives and friends, rather in the manner of her character drawing in her novels.

The parts of her life she shares most fully with her readers are her childhood and girlhood memories, the beginning of her literary career, her experiences as a volunteer nurse during the first world war, her travels, and her pleasant adventures as Max Mallowan's wife.

An Autobiography illuminates Agatha Christie's detective novels, in that the writer notes particular places she used for settings and individuals that led her to think of characters. She also explains attitudes that inform her detective fiction, such as her essentially Victorian social and moral conservatism, her views on the importance of discovering the guilty in order to protect the innocent, her notions on the built-in imbalance that keeps criminals from applying brakes as ordinary citizens do, and her scepticism about new ideologies for perfecting the human condition.

The connection between materials in *An Autobiography* and some of the Mary Westmacott novels is greater, but more complex. Most conspicuously in *Giant's Bread* and *Absent in the Spring*, novels written much earlier, the writer, as we have already suggested, uses material that would appear in *An Autobiography*. Sample parallel passages from *Giant's Bread* and *An Autobiography* reveal the general nature of such reuse.

For example, in *An Autobiography*, Agatha Christie describes a childhood fantasy. "Mrs. Green had a hundred children, of whom the important ones were Poodle, Squirrel and Tree. Those three accompanied me on all my exploits in the garden. They were not quite children and not quite dogs, but indeterminate kinds of creatures between the two" (*AA*, 11).

In *Giant's Bread*, published in 1930, or thirty-five years before the author finished writing *An Autobiography*, the central figure, Vernon, imagines a playmate named Mr. Green who had a hundred children. "The hundred, in Vernon's mind, were kept intact, a joyous mob

that raced down the yew alleys behind Vernon and Mr. Green. But
the three others were different. They were called by the three most
beautiful names that Vernon knew: Poodle, Squirrel and Tree."[3]

Similarly, in *An Autobiography*, the writer recalls Nursie, "a fixed
point, never changing" who was "a Bible Christian" (*AA*, 13). In the
novel, the memory appears in these terms: "And at the centre of this
realistic nursery universe, dominating everything, was Nurse herself.
Person No. I of Vernon's Trinity. . . . After Nurse, there was God.
God was also very real to Vernon, mainly because he bulked so largely
in Nurse's conversation."[4]

There are similar verbal parallels between *An Autobiography* and *Absent in the Spring*, but in that novel, as suggested earlier, Agatha
Christie makes more fundamental use of autobiographical material.
She assigns her central figure the stresses and emotional crises she ac-
knowledges only in bare summaries in the autobiography, and she
makes them the core of fictional developments.

Stylistically, *An Autobiography* has much in common with the author's fiction. She uses the same techniques of characterization and the
same sketchy but evocative method of describing places.

The most remarkable stylistic element of *An Autobiography* is, perhaps, Christie's use of a small cluster of emotive adjectives as touch-
stones, adjectives such as *frightening, fascinating, splendid*, and, most
conspicuously, *happy*. She writes, for instance, "I had a very happy
childhood" (*AA*, 30); "servants were, I think, actively happy" (*AA*,
16); "I was a happy person at this period" (*AA*, 197); "we had a
happy leave together" (*AA, 246); "*I had now written three books,
was happily married, and my heart's desire was to live in the country"
(*AA*, 269); "I usually feel happier either writing things in longhand
or typing them" (*AA*, 328); "we met quite happily" (*AA*, 332); "a
happy ending to our stay there" (*AA*, 346); "Max and I set off happily" (*AA*, 387); "I was very happy being with Max again" (*AA*,
400); "we had a happy few days on that little Serbian boat" (*AA*,
412); and so on. Such phraseology suggests no paucity of vocabulary.
Instead it reveals, rather touchingly, a special kind of attitude toward
experience. It is the voice of a person measuring life by moments in
which satisfaction and pleasure became recognizable and real.

Because of her capacity for using such words as *happy* with effect
and with point, Agatha Christie's *Autobiography* is a narrative with
real charm.

Chapter Twelve
Bits and Pieces

In addition to the kinds of writings Agatha Christie produced in quantity, she published a few miscellaneous works, interesting primarily because they illuminate tendencies latent in her better-known efforts.

At intervals throughout her life, she wrote occasional poems. Toward the end of her life, she produced one children's book of poems and short stories, and in 1930 and 1931 she collaborated on a novel and two radio scripts, since printed in novella form, with other members of the Detection Club.

These bits and pieces of literary activity warrant only limited attention, but each, in its way, rounds out our picture of her career.

Verse

Agatha Christie published two slim volumes of verse. The twenty-six poems in the 1924 *Road of Dreams*, with one addition, one omission, and a few minor changes in the order of poems, became volume 1 of her second collection, the 1973 *Poems*, which included a total of sixty-two poems.

Her verse claims attention mainly because she wrote it. None of her poems grips the imagination; none is likely to compel memorization. She seems to have written verse mainly as an outlet for the whimsical streak in her nature or else in response to loneliness or similar emotions.

In the best of the early poems, "A Masque from Italy," she invents a series of songs for Harlequin, Columbine, Pierrot, Pierrette, and Punchinello. In unaffected but evocative language, she develops the theme that magic and imagination both lure and endanger. Though she would take liberties with the Harlequin figure when she adapted him to detective fiction in the Harley Quin–Mr. Satterthwaite short stories, in the poems she accords him firmly traditional treatment.

Bittersweet moods generated by quasi-mythical material or by states of unfulfillment evidently attracted young Agatha Christie. She tried for this tone in several poems with themes of attraction-destruction. "Ballad of the Flint" recounts the story of a primitive British princess who kills a Viking stranger to satisfy her cultural role, then kills herself to join him in death. "Isolt of Brittany"—added to volume 1 in 1973—describes one whose thoughts remain fixed on someone elsewhere. In "Dark Sheila," a girl falls in love with a shadow lord, and in "The Princess Says," a mysterious lover comes from the South, then vanishes.

Except "Hymn to Ra," a chant celebrating a sense of cultural identity with metal, the other early poems all deal with yearning for children, death, dreams, or abstract nature.

Agatha Christie is sentimental, but she manages a little surprise in "Elizabeth of England" and "To a Beautiful Old Lady," two poems about the pathos of childlessness, and in "The Bells of Brittany," a poem about a child whose mother has died in childbirth. She is only conventionally sentimental in "A Passing," "Wild Roses," and "There Where My Lover Lies" and conventionally patriotic in "World Hymns 1914" and "Easter 1918."

"The Dream Spinners," "The Road of Dreams," and "The Dream City" define dreams as ways of knowing, and connect dreams, more or less, with awareness of death. These seem to be the earliest poems in the collection, for the writer depends heavily on adverbs such as *joyfully*, *defiantly*, and *courageously* and on rhetorical questions. She also resorts to odd capitalization, and her meters wobble.

The nature poems, "The Ballad of Maytime," "Down in the Wood," "Heritage," "Spring," "Young Morning," "A Palm Tree in the Desert," "Wild Roses," and "Progression," run to personifications and, despite a sweet girlishness of manner, all offer inescapably trite images.

Internal references and, indeed, dates in titles demonstrate that many of the poems in volume 2 were written in Agatha Christie's full maturity. But the general lack of development in her technical skills makes it difficult to guess the dates of composition of most of the verses, especially those like "Beauty," "The Water Flows," "A Wandering Tune," "An Island," "Undine," and "Enchantment." All these exhibit the impulse toward abstraction about emotions and external nature, or the penchant for fragmentary fairy-tale making of the volume 1 poems. One poem, "Count Fersen to the Queen," involves representation of ordinary human emotions in historical figures, rather in the manner of "Elizabeth of England."

In a few poems, namely "The Sculptor," "Ctesiphon," "In Bagh-dad," "To a Cedar Tree," "Hawthorne Trees in Spring," and "I Wore My New Canary Suit," Christie achieves a low-wattage jolt of surprise and recognition through her ideas, if not through her use of language. In "Racial Musings," a protest against the urge for sameness in people, Christie plays with internal rhyme (for example, "satiety but no variety"), but the last line, in capital letters, reads "A BORE. A BORE. A BORE." In "Picnic 1960" she contrives to be mildly amusing about dust and litter.

The most attractive verses in volume 2 are those clearly, or apparently, addressed to Max Mallowan. These include one Shakespearean sonnet, "To M. E. L. M. in Absence," in which the final couplet ends rather surprisingly with an ellipsis. "So in my winter, love, I dream of spring / Enclosed within the circle of your ring. . . . "[1] "What Is Love," "Remembrance," "A Choice," and "My Flower Garden" affectionately lament a loved one's absence. Key images in these verses, one suspects, are rather private in nature.

Three poems address children. "Calvary" may not seem quite a child's poem, but it first appeared, with minor differences, as "Gold, Frankincense and Myrrh" in *Star over Bethlehem*, as did "Jenny by the Sea." "From a Grown-up to a Child" offers whimsical reassurance that there must be good fairies.

Agatha Christie's poems never have received and probably never will receive, much critical attention. Inescapably minor as verse, they do give engaging, sometimes endearing, glimpses of an art at which the "sausage machine" of a detective novelist, who was given to quoting Shakespeare and Tennyson and who borrowed a title for a straight novel from T. S. Eliot, would evidently have liked to excel.

Star over Bethlehem

Admittedly, Max Mallowan never set himself up as a detached critic of his wife's work. Though obviously prejudiced in her favor, he nonetheless characterized her separate efforts perceptively.

Of the 1965 collection for children, *Star over Bethlehem*, which the writer signed Agatha Christie Mallowan, Professor Mallowan wrote: "Perhaps her most charming and among the most original of her works was a little series of religious stories written for Christmastide, entitled *Star over Bethlehem* (1965). These sweet tales have given unalloyed pleasure to many. They may fairly be styled 'Holy Detective Stories' "[2]

The six stories and five poems in *Star over Bethlehem*—especially the stories—though not, perhaps, easy reading for average children, charm because they are not quite predictable.

In the title story, for instance, Mary accepts her son's future despite Lucifer's tempting offer to take the Christ child back to God to prevent his pain. Somewhat similarly, in "The Naughty Donkey," the donkey, though troubled by a vision of what lay in store for the Christ child, still chooses to carry him and his mother to Egypt, asking only to be loved by him.

Another adaptation of biblical material occurs in "The Island," in which Mary treats the apostle John as a foster son until Christ comes for her and John takes on his mission.

In more modern settings, "The Water Bus" recounts the experiences of an inhibited, middle-class Englishwoman touched by Christ's cloak and moved to love people. "In the Cool of the Evening" sensitively treats the anguish of a couple over their retarded son, whose companion in the garden is God.

One story, "Promotion in the Highest," treats in prose the same idea as the poem before it, "The Saints of God." Both recount the adventures of saints plopped down in the year 2000 and obliged to repeat their earlier achievements.

The highly orthodox may well be startled by the stories, if not by the poems, in *Star over Bethlehem*. But the Christie story-telling gifts and her inventiveness with surprises are obvious, even when she writes for children.

Collaborations

In 1930 and 1931, Agatha Christie engaged in three exercises in collaboration with other members of the Detection Club, a group in which she may or may not have been an original member.[3] She helped to write two BBC radio scripts, *Behind the Screen* and *The Scoop*, first published in the BBC weekly periodical, *The Listener*, in 1930 and 1931 and reprinted in book form in 1983, and one collaborative novel, *The Floating Admiral*, first published in 1931 and reprinted in 1980.

In all three efforts, various members of the Detection Club contributed separate segments of the narratives, generally with limited knowledge of the plans of other contributors.

The best source of information about the radio scripts, Janet Morgan's biography of Christie, reveals that J. R. Ackerley, an assistant producer of BBC's Talk Department, directed both. Contributors to the six-part *Behind the Screen* included Hugh Walpole, Dorothy L. Sayers, Anthony Berkeley, E. C. Bentley, Ronald Knox, and Christie, who wrote the second segment of the story. Each contributor read his or her own chapter, and halfway through the series, the audience was invited to analyze suspects' motives and predict the outcome.

According to Morgan, despite Ackerley's efforts to keep the story thread cohesive, each contributor "made matters difficult" for the writer to follow by offering his own kind of clues and by practicing his own idiosyncratic style.[4] Christie marked her own contribution by playing with dialect in the servants' speech and by hinting that every member of the family in whose house the corpse appeared might be a suspect.

For the second BBC collaboration, *The Scoop*, broadcast in twelve weekly installments beginning in January 1931, Dorothy L. Sayers tried to organize matters a bit more clearly. Morgan, reporting that the writing team agreed to a rough plot outline and consulted with one another about details, reproduces fragments of correspondence between Sayers and Christie in which Sayers advises her colleague to ignore BBC injunctions about keeping the story thread minimal and proposes that the whole group withdraw if Ackerley continues to bother them.[5]

In addition to Agatha Christie, the writers participating in *The Scoop* included Dorothy L. Sayers, E. C. Bentley, Anthony Berkeley, Freeman Wills Crofts, and Clemence Dane. Mrs. Christie wrote the second and fourth installments, for which she was paid fifty guineas, just over half her standard fee for short stories. A note to Ackerley, reprinted in the Morgan biography, explains why *The Scoop* was her last collaborative radio effort. She wrote: "The truth of the matter is I hate writing short things and they really are *not* profitable. I don't mind an odd one now and again, but the energy to devise a series is much better employed in writing a couple of books. So there it is! With apologies."[6]

The first Christie chapter in *The Scoop* recounts inquest proceedings, and granting that collective works limited every writer's leeway in creating characters, its primary value lies in its rapid, generally comic revelation of witnesses' social attitudes. Her particular plot complication lies in her setting up a possibly overheard conversation.

Her second chapter involves dialogue between bright young things, rather in the manner of her early romance thrillers, and she plants a possible red herring about double identities for a suspect, and another clue about a man passing out religious pamphlets on a train platform.

Since the printed versions of *Behind the Screen* and *The Scoop* do not include appendices which indicate the solution each writer intended, one can only guess what Christie had in mind with the developments she built into her segments.

The 1931 collaborative novel, *The Floating Admiral* does include such information. The Christie solution offered is appreciably less complicated than that of some others, such as Sayers, and turns, as did many of those in the Christie detective novels, on a revelation of the personal pasts of characters.

Her chapter of the novel, entitled "Mainly Conversation," begins with speculation about the implications of costume. As in the radio scripts, Christie tends to concentrate on the characters and views of the servants, planting essentially domestic clues and rather ignoring her colleagues' openings for political conspiracies.

None of the collaborations has the sense of narrative direction any single contributor usually achieved in his or her own work. These exercises, in short, are only for real *aficionados* of classic detective fiction, those prepared to participate at second hand in the Detection Club's playful efforts to promote their special subgenre.

Agatha Christie's participation in these group activities is interesting primarily because it reveals a shy, "unclubbable" lady's good-humored willingness to join with others in promoting what Dorothy Sayers, in the introduction to *The Floating Admiral*, called primarily a game for members, an attempt to discover how cleverly they could solve problems they did not plan from the ending backward, the standard procedure of all classic detective writers.[7]

Chapter Thirteen
Conclusion

How important a writer was Agatha Christie? By quantitative measures—sales of books and box office demand for her plays, she may prove the best-selling writer in English in the twentieth century. Her books have outsold any other writer's, and *The Mousetrap* and *Witness for the Prosecution* have become transatlantic institutions. Agatha Christie has found a prodigious reading and play-going audience.

Measuring Agatha Christie qualitatively is more difficult. Despite her popular success, some of her writing is clearly trivial and some, after only half a century, seems extremely dated. No one, for instance, could take Christie seriously as a poet, and not all her prose merits close attention. Her romance thrillers seem either excessively arch or simply silly today, and her spy thrillers tend to be either preachy or absurd. For both kinds of thrillers, she contrived loose and incredible plots and settled for unconvincing, slang-filled dialogue.

Though uneven, her straight Mary Westmacott novels would seem to have a better chance of survival than her thrillers. *Absent in the Spring* and *Unfinished Portrait*, in particular, combine interesting narrative techniques and compelling story threads to produce firmly disciplined narratives. These novels merit larger audiences than either has in fact enjoyed. The other Westmacott novels, which mix occultism and frequently glib psychologizing, are less impressive.

The two Christie autobiographical books, *Come, Tell Me How You Live* and *An Autobiogrpahy*, are enormously attractive works. Both display the writer's narrative skill; both exhibit her singular personal charm. Yet Agatha Christie's reputation never depended on these efforts.

The Christie achievement must be measured by her whodunits. She dominated twentieth-century classic British detective fiction in all three of its forms: the short story, the novel, the play. As a mystery writer, she outproduced her rivals, even as she maintained an extraordinary level of worksmanship for over half a century.

Her detective fiction is outstanding, both for the variety she achieved within the form's rigorous rules for plot development, and for her invention of entertaining, if stylized, characters. Such fiction allows only one basic kind of resolution. The detective must discover who committed the crime and must explain away the puzzlement and misunderstanding the criminal managed to generate. With a Christie whodunit, a reader confidently anticipates an ending that will satisfy expectations, but he can count on being surprised by the manipulation of details that lead to that ending.

Agatha Christie's remarkable success in creating many plots of this type clearly depended on her ingenuity with mutations and permutations of basic patterns. As we have seen, she constantly reused situations, characters, clusters of characters, and settings. But she made her tales seem fresh by varying at least one basic narrative element from work to work. If she reused a situation, she modified characters. If she reused characters, she put them in new settings. When she expanded a short story into a novel or adapted a story or novel for the stage, she often changed her original ending. No other writer of this century has so fully understood the craft of combining and recombining, to give readers a familiar, yet new, imaginative experience.

In short, she perfected the art of plotting, while her "serious" contemporaries shied away from plot as an oversimplification of the complexities of experience.

Further, as other twentieth-century writers began to avoid highly typed, externalized characters, Agatha Christie polished the art of creating them. Though others subscribed, perhaps hastily, to E. M. Forster's dicta about round characters and flat characters, and generally accepted the view that flat characters lack interest and significance, Christie specialized in creating figures readily identifiable by their manners and their social or personal quirks, figures belonging to the grand tradition of eighteenth-and nineteenth-century British fiction, the tradition of Fielding, Smollett, Austen, and Dickens. Christie peopled her mystery tales with figures whose manners, dress, and speech invited readers to label them according to their social identities and personal quirks. These characters rarely, perhaps never, reveal new dimensions of human nature. Instead they suggest that an understanding of individuals, whatever social microcosms they occupy, is merely a matter of recognizing what types of people they are.

This comedy-of-manners approach to characterization in Agatha Christie's mystery tales sets up a comedy-of-manners approach to social history, one that focuses on little details of life-style. Christie may have seen the folkways of the British upper-middle-class more

Also available from Twayne's Authors Series:

P. D. James by Richard B. Gidez
Dorothy L. Sayers by Mary Brian Durkin, O. P.
Dashiell Hammett by William Marling
John D. MacDonald by Edgar Hirshberg
Graham Greene by A. A. DeVitis

nostalgically than most of her contemporaries did, but she obviously drew her settings from observed places and people. And with her specificity about manners, Christie entices willing suspension of disbelief in the kinds of characters and the kinds of situations she invents. She also recorded a time and a place convincingly. Conceivably, future generations may use her works as a source of social history, as twentieth-century social historians now use the writings of Smollett and Trollope.

Finally, the fact that the distinguishing techniques of Agatha Christie's whodunits are out of step with current practices may, paradoxically, represent the most significant aspect of her career. The extraordinary popularity of her works suggests that there are still readers drawn to plot and to typed characters, as well as to the recording of social history. Her works demonstrate the fact that the traditional elements of fiction have vitality in them yet. Because she embued her mystery making with this vitality, Agatha Christie, who modestly saw herself as a literary sausage maker, may claim a more important place in literary history than she seemed ever to expect. In her subgenera, she kept alive elements of the grand tradition in British novel writing.

Notes and References

Chapter One

1. Gwen Robyns, *The Mystery of Agatha Christie* (Garden City, N.Y.: Doubleday & Co., 1978), 12.
2. Agatha Christie, *An Autobiography* (New York: Dodd, Mead & Co., 1977), 18. Hereafter cited in the text as *AA*.
3. Robyns, *Mystery*, 75–85.
4. Ibid., 82–83.
5. Janet Morgan, *Agatha Christie: A Biography* (London: Collins, 1984), 158–59.
6. Max Mallowan, *Mallowan's Memoirs* (New York: Dodd, Mead & Co., 1977), 44.
7. Robyns, *Mystery*, 114.
8. Morgan, *Biography*, 268.

Chapter Two

1. Janet Morgan identifies this story as "The House of Beauty," published as "The House of Dreams" in the January 1926 issue of *Sovereign Magazine*. See Morgan, *Biography*, 48–49.
2. Two unanthologized stories are "The Harlequin's Tea Set," published in *Winter's Crimes, 3* (1971) and in Ellery Queen's *Murdercade* (1975), and "The House of Dreams," cited above. The six stories for children in *Star over Bethlehem* are not included in this count.
3. Charles Osborne, *The Life and Crimes of Agatha Christie* (New York: Holt, Rinehart & Winston, 1982), 50–51.
4. Agatha Christie, *Partners in Crime* (New York: Berkley Books, 1984), 75.
5. Agatha Christie, *The Tuesday Club Murders* (New York: Dell, 1967), 53.
6. Dennis Sanders and Len Lovallo, *The Agatha Christie Companion: A Complete Guide to Agatha Christie's Life and Work* (New York: Delacorte Press, 1984), 99.
7. Morgan, *Biography*, 49.
8. *Times Literary Supplement*, 7 July 1934.
9. Morgan, *Biography*, 224.
10. Agatha Christie, *The Labors of Hercules* (New York: Dell, 1982), 5–6.

146 AGATHA CHRISTIE

11. Earl F. Bargainnier, *The Gentle Art of Murder: The Detective Fiction of Agatha Christie* (Bowling Green, Ohio: Bowling Green University Popular Press, 1980), 124–25.

12. Morgan, *Biography*, 324.

13. H. Douglas Thomson, *Masters of Mystery: A Study of the Detective Story* (London: William Collins Sons & Co., 1931), 208.

Chapter Three

1. W. H. Auden, "The Guilty Vicarage," in *The Dyer's Hand and Other Essays* (New York: Random House, 1948). Reprinted in *Detective Fiction: A Collection of Critical Essays,* ed. Robin W. Winks (Englewood Cliffs, N. J.: Prentice-Hall, 1980), 15.

2. Hanna Chaney, *The Detective Novel of Manners: Hedonism, Morality, and the Life of Reason* (Rutherford, N. J.: Fairleigh Dickinson Univ. Press, 1981), 16–21.

3. See "A Detective Story Decalogue" and "The Detection Club Oath" in *The Art of the Detective Story*, ed. Howard Haycraft (New York: Simon & Schuster, 1946), 194–99.

4. Agatha Christie, *The Pale Horse* (New York: Pocket Books, 1962), 9.

5. Chaney, *Detective Novel of Manners*, 79–91.

6. Dorothy L. Sayers, "Aristotle on Detective Fiction," in *Unpopular Opinions* (London: Victor Gollancz, 1946), 178–90. Reprinted in *Detective Fiction*, ed. Robin W. Winks (Englewood Cliffs, N. J.: Prentice-Hall, 1980) 25–34.

7. Auden, "Guilty Vicarage," 24.

8. David I. Grossvogel, "Agatha Christie: Containment of the Unknown," in *The Poetics of Murder: Detective Fiction and Literary Theory,* ed. Glenn W. Most and William W. Stowe (San Diego: Harcourt, Brace, Jovanovich, 1983), 253.

9. Ernest Mandel, *Delightful Murder: A Social History of the Crime Story* (London: Pluto Press, 1984), 16.

10. Stephen Knight, *Form and Ideology in Crime Fiction* (Bloomington: Indiana Univ. Press, 1980), 108–9.

11. Agatha Christie, *The Mysterious Affair at Styles* (New York: Bantam Books, 1961), 117.

12. Knight, *Form and Ideology,* 123.

13. Agatha Christie, *The Murder of Roger Ackroyd* (New York: Pocket Books, 1939), 17, 11, 39, 25.

Chapter Four

1. Morgan, *Biography,* 201–4.

2. *Times Literary Supplement,* 27 October 1934.

3. Charles Osborne, *The Life and Crimes of Agatha Christie* (New York: Holt, Rinehart & Winston, 1982), 84.

4. Agatha Christie, *Murder in Three Acts (Three-Act Tragedy)* (New York: Popular Library, 1977), 175.

5. Julian Symon, *Bloody Murder: From the Detective Story to the Crime Novel: A History* (Harmondsworth: Penguin Books, 1974), 135.

6. Agatha Christie, *Murder in Mesopotamia,* in *Spies Among Us* (New York: Dodd, Mead & Co., 1968), 355, 386, 381.

7. Agatha Christie, *The ABC Murders,* in *Surprise Endings by Hercule Poirot* (New York: Dodd, Mead & Co., n.d.), 8.

8. In *Come, Tell Me How You Live,* the author expresses admiration for the Yezidis, the worshippers of Shaitan, and for their holy shrine. (New York: Pocket Books, 1977), 115.

9. Mallowan, *Memoirs,* 212.

10. Agatha Christie, *Cards on the Table,* in *Surprise Endings,* 348.

11. Agatha Christie, *Death on the Nile* (New York: Bantam Books, 1971), 45–46.

12. Agatha Christie, *Appointment with Death,* in *Make Mine Murder!* (New York: Dodd, Mead & Co., 1962), 63.

13. Osborne, *Life and Crimes,* 105–6.

14. Morgan, *Biography,* 214.

15. Agatha Christie, *A Holiday for Murder (Murder for Christmas)* (New York: Bantam Books, 1969), n.p.

16. Sanders and Lovallo, *Companion,* 168.

Chapter Five

1. Osborne, *Life and Crimes,* 113.

2. Francis Wyndham, "The Algebra of Agatha Christie" (London) *Sunday Times,* 1966 February 27. Cited in Osborne, *Life and Crimes*, 207.

3. John G. Cawelti, *Adventure, Mystery, and Romance* (Chicago: Univ. of Chicago Press, 1976), 111–18.

4. Agatha Christie, *Evil Under the Sun* (New York: Pocket Books, 1969), 38.

5. Morgan, *Biography,* 222.

6. Osborne, *Life and Crimes,* 129.

7. Agatha Christie, *Towards Zero* (New York: Pocket Books, 1969), 3.

8. Robyns, *Mystery,* 124.

Chapter Six

1. Agatha Christie, *There Is a Tide (Taken at the Flood)* (New York: Dell, 1974), 149–50.

2. Agatha Christie, *Crooked House* (New York: Dodd, Mead & Co., 1949), 89.

3. Agatha Christie, *A Murder Is Announced* (New York: Pocket Books, 1972), 85.

4. Agatha Christie, *Blood Will Tell (Mrs. McGinty's Dead)* (New York: Walter J. Black, 1951), 89.

5. Ibid.

6. Agatha Christie, *They Do It with Mirrors* (New York: Dodd, Mead & Co., Greenway Edition, 1952), 120.

7. *New York Times,* 15 March 1953.

8. Agatha Christie, *After the Funeral (Funerals Are Fatal)* (New York: Pocket Books, 1975), 149.

Chapter Seven

1. See reviews quoted in Sanders and Lovallo, *Companion,* 304.

2. Sanders and Lovallo, *Companion,* 315.

3. Agatha Christie, *The Mirror Crack'd* (New York: Pocket Books, 1972), 11.

4. Agatha Christie, *The Clocks* (New York: Pocket Books, 1976), 117.

5. Agatha Christie, *A Caribbean Mystery* (New York: Dodd, Mead & Co., 1964), 2–3.

6. Sanders and Lovallo, *Companion,* 334–35.

7. Agatha Christie, *At Bertram's Hotel* (New York: Dodd, Mead & Co., 1965), 195.

8. Sanders and Lovallo, *Companion,* 342–43; Mallowan, *Memoirs,* 206.

9. Cited in Osborne, *Life and Crimes,* 214.

10. Mandel, *Delightful Murder,* 29.

11. Knight, *Form and Ideology,* 111.

12. Emma Lathen, "Cornwallis's Revenge," in *Agatha Christie: First Lady of Crime,* ed. H. R. F. Keating (New York: Holt, Rinehart & Winston, 1977), 90–91.

Chapter Eight

1. Agatha Christie, *The Secret Adversary* (New York: Bantam Books, 1970), 202.

2. Ibid., 75–76.

3. Agatha Christie, *The Secret of Chimneys* (New York: Dell, 1979), 118.

4. Ibid., 153.

5. Bargainnier, *Gentle Art,* 85.

6. Agatha Christie, *Passenger to Frankfurt* (New York: Pocket Books, 1972), x.

7. Morgan, *Biography*, 362.
8. Ibid., 363.
9. Ibid., 364.
10. Ibid., 371–72.

Chapter Nine

1. Morgan, *Biography*, 287.
2. *Giant's Bread*, in *The Mary Westmacott-Christie Reader* (New York: Arbor House, n.d.), 8.
3. Morgan, *Biography*, 168–69.
4. Mallowan, *Memoirs*, 195.
5. Dorothy B. Hughes, "The Christie Nobody Knew," in *First Lady of Crime*, 124.
6. Hughes, "Nobody Knew," 128.
7. Morgan, *Biography*, 305.
8. Ibid., 305.
9. Ibid., 305.
10. Hughes, "Nobody Knew," 123–24.

Chapter Ten

1. Robert Graves, "After a Century, Will Anyone Care Whodunit," *New York Times Book Review*, 25 August 1957.
2. Sanders and Lovallo, *Companion*, 399–425.
3. Mallowan, *Memoirs*, 219.
4. Osborne, *Life and Crimes*, 100–1.
5. Morgan, *Biography*, 286–87.
6. Sanders and Lovallo, *Companion*, 407–9.
7. *Times* (London), 20 March 1946.
8. *Times* (London), 8 June 1951.
9. Peter Saunders, *The Mousetrap Man* (London: Collins, 1972), 138.
10. Morgan, *Biography*, 262.
11. Osborne, *Life and Crimes*, 173.
12. Morgan, *Biography*, 285.
13. Osborne, *Life and Crimes*, 186.
14. Sanders and Lovallo, *Companion*, 422.
15. Ibid., 423.
16. J. C. Trewin, "A Midas Gift to the Theatre," in *First Lady of Crime*, 140.

Chapter Eleven

1. Agatha Christie, *Come, Tell Me How You Live* (New York: Pocket Books, 1977), 14. Hereafter cited in the text as *Live*.

2. Robyns, *Mystery,* 13, 94.
3. Agatha Christie, *Giant's Bread* (New York: Dell Books, 1975), 14.
4. Ibid., 15.

Chapter Twelve

1. Agatha Christie, *Poems* (London: Collins, 1973), 110.
2. Mallowan, *Memoirs,* 204.
3. Robyns, *Mystery,* 103; Morgan, *Biography,* 259.
4. Morgan, *Biography,* 195.
5. Ibid., 196.
6. Ibid., 198.
7. Dorothy L. Sayers, introduction to *The Floating Admiral* (New York: Charter Books, 1980), 4–5.

Selected Bibliography

PRIMARY SOURCES

1. Short Story Collections
   The Adventure of the Christmas Pudding. 1960.
   Dead Man's Mirror. See *Murder in the Mews.*
   Double Sin. 1961.
   The Golden Ball. 1971.
   The Hound of Death. 1933.
   The Labours of Hercules. 1947.
   The Listerdale Mystery. 1934.
   Miss Marple's Final Cases. 1979.
   The Mousetrap. See *Three Blind Mice.*
   Murder in the Mews, or *Dead Man's Mirror.* 1937.
   The Mysterious Mr. Quin. 1930.
   Parker Pyne Investigates, or *Mr. Parker Pyne, Detective.* 1934.
   Partners in Crime. 1929.
   Poirot Investigates. 1925.
   Poirot's Early Cases, or *Hercule Poirot's Early Cases.* 1974.
   The Regatta Mystery. 1939.
   The Thirteen Problems, or *The Tuesday Club Murders.* 1932.
   Three Blind Mice, or *The Mousetrap.* 1950.
   The Tuesday Club Murders. See *The Thirteen Problems.*
   The Under Dog. 1951.
   Witness for the Prosecution. 1948.
2. Detective Novels
   The ABC Murders. 1936.
   After the Funeral, or *Funerals Are Fatal.* 1953.
   And Then There Were None. See *Ten Little Niggers.*
   Appointment with Death. 1938.
   At Bertram's Hotel. 1965.
   The Big Four. 1927.
   Blood Will Tell. See *Mrs. McGinty's Dead.*
   The Body in the Library. 1942.
   The Boomerang Clue. See *Why Didn't They Ask Evans?*
   Cards on the Table. 1936.
   A Caribbean Mystery. 1964.

Cat among the Pigeons. 1959.
The Clocks. 1963.
Crooked House, 1949.
Curtain. 1975.
Dead Man's Folly. 1956.
Death Comes at the End. 1944.
Death in the Air. See *Death in the Clouds.*
Death in the Clouds, or *Death in the Air.* 1935.
Death on the Nile. 1937.
Dumb Witness, or *Poirot Loses a Client.* 1937.
Easy to Kill. See *Murder Is Easy.*
Elephants Can Remember. 1972.
Endless Night. 1967.
Evil under the Sun. 1941.
Five Little Pigs, or *Murder in Retrospect.* 1943.
The Floating Admiral. By Agatha Christie and others. 1931.
4:50 from Paddington, or *What Mrs. McGillicuddy Saw.* 1957.
Funerals Are Fatal. See *After the Funeral.*
Hallowe'en Party. 1969.
Hercule Poirot's Christmas, or *Murder for Christmas.* 1938.
Hickory Dickory Death. See *Hickory Dickory Dock.*
Hickory Dickory Dock, or *Hickory Dickory Death.* 1955.
The Hollow, or *Murder after Hours.* 1946.
Lord Edgware Dies, or *Thirteen at Dinner.* 1933.
The Man in the Brown Suit. 1924.
The Mirror Crack'd. See *The Mirror Crack'd from Side to Side.*
The Mirror Crack'd from Side to Side, or *The Mirror Crack'd.* 1962.
The Moving Finger. 1942.
Mrs. McGinty's Dead, or *Blood Will Tell.* 1952.
Murder after Hours. See *The Hollow.*
Murder at Hazelmoor. See *The Sittaford Mystery.*
The Murder at the Vicarage. 1930.
Murder for Christmas. See *Hercule Poirot's Christmas.*
Murder in Mesopotamia. 1936.
Murder in Retrospect. See *Five Little Pigs.*
Murder in the Calais Coach. See *Murder on the Orient Express.*
Murder in Three Acts. See *Three-Act Tragedy.*
A Murder Is Announced. 1950.
Murder Is Easy, or *Easy to Kill.* 1939.
The Murder of Roger Ackroyd. 1926.
Murder on the Links. 1923.
Murder on the Orient Express, or *Murder in the Calais Coach.* 1934.
Murder with Mirrors. See *They Do It with Mirrors.*

The Mysterious Affair at Styles. 1920.
The Mystery of the Blue Train. 1928.
Nemesis. 1971.
One, Two, Buckle My Shoe, or *The Patriotic Murders.* 1940.
Ordeal by Innocence. 1958.
The Pale Horse. 1961.
The Patriotic Murders. See *One, Two, Buckle My Shoe.*
Peril at End House. 1932.
A Pocket Full of Rye. 1953.
Poirot Loses a Client. See *Dumb Witness.*
Remembered Death. See *Sparkling Cyanide.*
Sad Cypress. 1940.
The Sittaford Mystery, or *Murder at Hazelmoor.* 1931.
Sleeping Murder. 1976.
Sparkling Cyanide, or *Remembered Death.* 1945.
Taken at the Flood, or *There Is a Tide.* 1948.
Ten Little Indians. See *Ten Little Niggers.*
Ten Little Niggers, or *Ten Little Indians,* or *And Then There Were None.*
    1939.
There Is a Tide. See *Taken at the Flood.*
They Do It with Mirrors, or *Murder with Mirrors.* 1952.
Third Girl. 1966.
Thirteen at Dinner. See *Lord Edgware Dies.*
Three-Act Tragedy, or *Murder in Three Acts.* 1934.
Towards Zero. 1944.
What Mrs. McGillicuddy Saw. See *4:50 from Paddington.*
Why Didn't They Ask Evans? or *The Boomerang Clue.* 1934.

3. Romance and Spy Thrillers
    Destination Unknown, or *So Many Steps to Death.* 1954.
    N or M? 1941.
    Passenger to Frankfurt: An Extravaganza. 1970.
    Postern of Fate. 1973.
    The Secret Adversary. 1922.
    The Secret of Chimneys. 1925.
    The Seven Dials Mystery. 1929.
    So Many Steps to Death. See *Destination Unknown.*
    They Came to Baghdad. 1951.

4. Mary Westmacott Novels
    Absent in the Spring. 1944.
    The Burden. 1956.
    A Daughter's a Daughter. 1952.

Giant's Bread, 1930.
The Rose and the Yew Tree. 1947.
Unfinished Portrait. 1934.

5. Plays
   a. Written or adapted by Christie herself
   Akhnaton. Written 1937; published 1973; never performed.
   Appointment with Death. 1945.
   Black Coffee. 1930.
   Fiddlers Three. 1972.
   Go Back for Murder. 1960.
   The Hollow. 1951.
   The Mousetrap. 1952.
   Murder on the Nile. 1945.
   Rule of Three. Includes *The Rats, Afternoon at the Seaside, The Patient*. 1962.
   Spider's Web. 1954.
   Ten Little Niggers, or *Ten Little Indians*. 1945.
   Towards Zero. Adapted in collaboration with Gerald Verner, 1956.
   The Unexpected Guest. 1958.
   Verdict. 1958.
   Witness for the Prosecution. 1953.
   b. Adapted by others from Christie's work
   Alibi. Michael Morton. 1928.
   Cards on the Table. Leslie Darbon. 1981.
   Love from a Stranger. Frank Vosper. 1936.
   Murder at the Vicarage. Moie Charles and Barbara Toy, 1949.
   A Murder Is Announced. Leslie Darbon. 1977.
   Peril at End House. Arnold Ridley. 1940.

6. Autobiographical Writings
   An Autobiography. 1977.
   Come, Tell Me How You Live. 1946.

7. Verse
   Poems. 1973.
   The Road of Dreams, Included in *Poems*. 1924.

8. Children's Book
   Star Over Bethlehem. 1965.

9. Radio Scripts
   "Three Blind Mice." 1947.
   "Behind the Screen." In collaboration. 1930.
   "The Scoop." In collaboration. 1931.

SECONDARY SOURCES

1. Biographical

Mallowan, Max. *Mallowan's Memoirs.* London: Collins, 1977. Graceful autobiography. Rich in details about Agatha Christie's personality, her working methods, and sources.

Morgan, Janet. *Agatha Christie: A Biography.* London: Collins, 1984. The biography authorized by Christie's family. Especially valuable for Christie's writing notebooks and personal correspondence. The definitive biography.

Robyns, Gwen. *The Mystery of Agatha Christie.* Garden City, N.Y.: Doubleday & Co., 1978. Without access to personal records made available to Janet Morgan, a biography offering a judicious view of the writer's personality and career.

2. Critical and Historical

Bargainnier Earl F. *The Gentle Art of Murder: The Detective Fiction of Agatha Christie.* Bowling Green, Ohio: Bowling Green Univ. Popular Press, 1980. A perceptive analysis focusing on techniques and social attitudes.

Barnard, Robert. *A Talent to Deceive: An Appreciation of Agatha Christie.* New York: Dodd, Mead & Co., 1980. An important critical analysis focusing on literary methods of Christie's detective fiction.

Cawelti, John G. *Adventure, Mystery, and Romance: Formula Stories as Art and Popular Culture.* Chicago: Univ. of Chicago Press, 1976. A seminal study of formulaic fiction, offering detailed comment on several Christie novels.

Chaney, Hanna. *The Detective Novel of Manners: Hedonism, Morality, and the Life of Reason.* Rutherford, N.J.: Fairleigh Dickinson Univ. Press, 1981. An analysis of detective fiction's roots in the nineteenth-century novel-of-manners tradition. Comments on several Christie novels.

Grella, George. "Murder and Manners: The Formal Detective Novel." *Novel,* 4 (1970): 30–48. A fresh analysis, which prompted the Chaney study, among others.

Grossvogel, David I. *Mystery and Its Fictions: From Oedipus to Agatha Christie.* Baltimore: Johns Hopkins Univ. Press, 1979. A sweeping theoretical study, with a full chapter on Christie's methods.

Haycraft, Howard. *Murder for Pleasure: The Life and Times of the Detective Story.* London: Peter Davies, 1942. A standard historical study of the form.

Haycraft, Howard, ed. *The Art of the Mystery Story: A Collection of Critical Essays.* New York: Appleton-Century-Crofts, 1941. A convenient anthology of some of the best essays on detective fiction; especially valuable for study of Christie.

H. R. F. Keating. *Agatha Christie: First Lady of Crime.* London: Weidenfeld & Nicolson, 1977. A miscellaneous collection of short essays on various aspects of Christie's career. Several essays, notably that of Emma Lathen, clever and full of insight. Heavily illustrated.

Knight, Stephen. *Form and Ideology in Crime Fiction.* Bloomington: Indiana Univ. Press, 1980. A study focusing on social attitudes in detective fiction. Fairly extensive commentary on Christie.

Mandel, Ernest. *Delightful Murder: A Social History of the Crime Story.* London: Pluto Press, 1984. A thoughtful Marxist analysis of Christie's fiction.

Most, Glenn W., and William W. Stowe. *Poetics of Murder: Detective Fiction and Literary Theory.* San Diego: Harcort Brace Jovanovich, 1983. An anthology of critical essays on the form.

Murch, A. E. *The Development of the Detective Novel.* London: Peter Owen, 1958. A historical review of the development of the form.

Osborne, Charles. *The Life and Crimes of Agatha Christie.* New York: Holt, Rinehart & Winston, 1982. A comprehensive review of Christie's works, with sample critical responses to each.

Palmer, Jerry. *Thrillers: Genesis and Structure of a Popular Genre.* New York: St. Martin's Press, 1979. A compact history of the development of the subgenera.

Porter, Dennis. *The Pursuit of Crime: Art and Ideology in Detective Fiction.* New Haven: Yale Univ. Press, 1981. An exploration of recurring ideas in detective fiction.

Radine, Serge. *Quelques Aspects du Roman policier psychologique.* (Some aspects of the psychological police novel.) Geneva: Editions du Mont-Blanc, 1960. A classic study of the development of detective fiction.

Sanders, Dennis, and Len Lovallo. *The Christie Companion: The Complete Guide to Agatha Christie's Life and Work.* New York: Delacorte Press, 1984. A study, similar to Osborne's, that examines all of Christie's writings. A necessary tool for study of the author.

Saunders, Peter. *The Mousetrap Man.* London: Collins, 1972. Memoirs of the producer of most of Christie's plays; valuable for reminiscences about the writer for details about her stagecraft.

Scott, Sutherland. *Blood in Their Ink: The March of the Modern Mystery Novel.* London: Stanley Paul & Co., 1953. A brief and general review of the form.

Symons, Julian. *Mortal Consequences: A History—From the Detective Story to the Crime Novel.* New York: Harper & Row, 1972. Brief essays on the historical development of detective fiction.

Thomson, H. Douglas. *Masters of Mystery: A Study of the Detective Story.* London: William Collins, 1931. A detailed but somewhat dated history of the form.

Toye, Randall. *The Agatha Christie Who's Who.* New York: Holt, Rinehart & Winston, 1980. A dictionary of Christie's characters.

Watson, Colin. *Snobbery with Violence: Crime Stories and Their Audience.* London: Eyre & Spottiswoode, 1971. A clever analysis of the social presuppositions of classic British detective fiction.

Winks, Robin W. *Detective Fiction: A Collection of Critical Essays.* Englewood Cliffs, N.J.: Prentice-Hall, 1980. An anthology of essays on detective fiction, including the most important essays on the subject in this century.

Winn, Dilys. *Murderess Ink: The Better Half of the Mystery.* New York: Workman Publishing, 1979. A heavily illustrated, highly informal collection of trivia about many writers of detective fiction, including Agatha Christie.

Index

DATE DUE

GAYLORD			PRINTED IN U.S.A.